CONTENTS

Grade 3

Acting Exams

A Teacher's Guide

The
Playing
Space

Acting Exams

A Teacher's Guide

Games and exercises for teachers preparing students for LAMDA exams

VOLUME 1: GRADES 1–3

Consultant editor: Kerry Woods, BA (Hons), PGCE, PGC (Acting), LLAM

First published in Great Britain in 2016
by
The Playing Space
5 Bridge Road,
London N22 7SN
United Kingdom

ISBN 978-1-5233-0077-8

Acting Exams: A Teacher's Guide, Volume 1
Consultant editor: Kerry Woods
Copyright © The Playing Space 2016

theplayingspace.co.uk/books/
books@theplayingspace.co.uk

Cover photograph © Jan Klaas Kollhof

From a very young age, the games children play, both with each other and with adults, involve make-believe: pretend the spoonful of food is a train going into a tunnel; pretend the cuddly toys can talk; pretend I'm Batman and you're Spiderman. Yet as they settle into school life, opportunities for freewheeling imaginative play become limited. Increasingly, children have to satisfy the adult expectations that they are sensible and logical.

As a drama teacher, you offer an environment in which children needn't be sensible or logical but can imagine themselves and each other into weird lives and crazy situations. In a well run drama class, youngsters feel able to speak honestly without fearing that they will be told to be quiet or stop being silly. Drama pays attention to our feelings and how they are expressed, so it unclogs the channel between the inner and outer life, reconnecting how we feel with what we say and do. Good drama classes boost confidence, improve communication skills and promote teamwork. Drama also allows children to be children – exuberant, silly, spontaneous and joyful.

So why, you might ask, ruin all this by imposing an examination on young actors?! Aren't they tested enough as it is? Can you even mark an acting performance? Is there a right and a wrong way of doing a scene? Doesn't taking an exam suck all the joy out of acting?

One answer is that life is not an endless rehearsal. There are times when everyone has to stand up, often alone, and perform – in the school assembly, in the university interview, at the training conference. Entering your young students for a LAMDA exam takes your drama from the cosy confines of the class out into the world. Many will feel pressure and nerves, but if you have prepared them well, they will do well, and the feeling of achievement will be immense. Performance situations will not seem so daunting after all.

Furthermore, teaching to the LAMDA Performance syllabus can give shape and structure to your lessons. To succeed in a LAMDA Acting exam, students must be able to interpret a dramatic text, both on its surface and within its deeper meaning. They must speak confidently and clearly. They must find ways of adapting and controlling the voice and body to give and sustain the illusion of an imagined world. They must understand and be able to discuss their creative process. They must become storytellers. Therefore, by working to the syllabus, you will be teaching the essential skills of an actor.

If drama classes are purely coaching sessions for exams, they might well be joyless. Yet preparing two acting scenes is an extended creative project (LAMDA suggests 20 Guided Learning Hours for Grade 1 Solo Acting). If your students feel that they are taking on a project, all of the work will have value for them, and the exam score will be just one part of the achievement.

This book, then, contains the blueprints for sixty creative projects, sixty journeys that will follow different paths and have different outcomes for every student who embarks upon them. There will be many unexpected twists and turns along the way, but I have no doubt that you will all enjoy the ride!

January 2016

Structure

Students taking a LAMDA exam in Acting at Grades 1–5 perform two scenes. One is of their own choosing, the other a set scene. All the set scenes are published in the *LAMDA Acting Anthology, Volume 3*. This book is a teacher's companion to the Acting Anthology.

This, the first volume of *Acting Exams: A Teacher's Guide,* provides resources for teachers preparing students for Acting exams at Grades 1–3. The second volume is for teachers preparing students for Grades 4 and 5.

This book follows the order of the Acting Anthology. Scenes are divided by grade. Within each grade are ten solo scenes and ten duologues. For each scene, this book provides a two-page chapter of teaching ideas. At the front of each grade section are two pages describing how the exam works at that grade. A table showing the assessment criteria and mark scheme is accompanied by an explanation of the structure of the exam and a checklist. The checklist helps teachers to ensure that they and their students are covering all the requirements for the exam. It is annotated with references to teaching ideas that appear throughout the book. These ideas can be cross-referenced in the index.

Supporting Material Available Online

A larger version of the grade checklist – which can be handed out for use at home or in class – is one of the many downloadable resources available on the web page which accompanies this book. You can find the resources at:

theplayingspace.co.uk/books/

This web page is a drama teacher's gateway to a range of materials which support the teaching ideas covered in this book. These materials include texts of the sources for scenes in the Acting Anthology, worksheets and other handouts, teaching materials, ideas for games, links to useful web sites and much more. Wherever the symbol to the left appears in the margin of this book, relevant supporting material can be found on the web page above.

Using This Book

This book does not give lesson plans. The games and exercises are suggestions, designed to inspire a teacher when planning a class. They offer ways of approaching a rehearsal session other than just 'taking it from the top'. They help a teacher to bring the scene to life, so that students can believe in the character and situation and imagine themselves there.

The exercises may be adapted and combined in any number of different ways. A teacher using this book might have a single student, a pair or a group. Students might be working towards the same grade or different grades. Wherever possible, we have suggested ways of adapting a solo exercise to suit a group and vice versa, turning a quick opener into an extended activity, adding a competitive element to a character study and other modifications.

Source Texts, Feature Boxes and Project Work

Nearly half of the scenes in the Acting Anthology are adapted from other sources, chiefly novels. Where a scene has been adapted from a novel, the chapter provides information about the source, an indication of where in the source the original episode appears and a brief sketch of the context. If a source text is out of copyright, our web page (see above) includes a copy of the relevant text as well as a link to a version that is publicly available online.

Roughly half the chapters in this book include a Feature Box. These sidebars explore fundamental teaching themes (animal characters; mime); principles (working safely online; looking after your examiner) and exercises (hot seating; command games) that have general application for any drama class as well as specific relevance for the scene under discussion. In the index, boldfaced page numbers refer to a Feature Box.

Every article includes a list of suggestions for Project Work – creative study, research and background tasks that will help your student to make acting choices when it is his or her turn to take the stage. In a group, Project Work can be set as homework or carried out in a quiet corner of the drama room while you rehearse with a different student.

Essential Equipment

Many of the exercises in this book require certain straightforward pieces of kit (which should, in any case, be in any drama teacher's tool bag):

- **tambourine** or similiar item for getting attention, making a signal and beating time
- **ball** or similar item for rolling, throwing and catching
- **stopwatch**
- several sets of **numbered cards** from 1–10
- **blindfolds**
- **art materials:** paper, colouring pens, scissors, glue, etc
- **magazines** in different styles and covering different subjects (for collages)

A Note on Gender and Pronouns

Many of the scenes in the Acting Anthology are unisex (the characters could be either male or female). Even where a character has a female name, you may cast a boy and make the character male as long as no words spoken by the character contradict this choice. In stage directions (not in the actual lines), *she* may be changed to *he* and vice versa.

Even if a character is emphatically and unambiguously female, a boy may play the part as a girl (and girls may play boys). If you do have a boy playing Jane Eyre or a girl playing Tom Sawyer, make sure that you and your student can give a good reason for choosing the scene.

Where a character is clearly masculine or clearly feminine, this book assumes casting to gender and uses the appropriate pronoun (*he* or *she*). For unisex scenes, because it is cumbersome to keep using *he/she* and *his/her* we plump for one or the other. So around half the chapters on unisex scenes use a masculine pronoun, around half a feminine pronoun. Teachers will use their common sense to see beyond the pronouns.

INTERPRETATION – 20 marks for each scene (40 total)
L01 Perform two scenes from memory, demonstrating an understanding of the material.

Does your student…	Pass	Merit	Distinction
Understand the MEANING of the words she is speaking?	Some	Most	All
Communicate the meaning of the words?	Some	Most	All
Understand the CHARACTER and the SITUATION?	Some of the time	Most of the time	All of the time
Communicate the character and the situation?	Some of the time	Most of the time	All of the time
Know the LINES?	Quite well	Well	Perfectly
Stay IMMERSED in the imaginary world?	Some of the time	Most of the time	Throughout

TECHNIQUE – 20 marks for each scene (40 total)
L02 Use vocal skills in response to the text.
L03 Use the performance space in response to the text.

Does your student…	Pass	Merit	Distinction
PROJECT (speak clearly and with appropriate volume)?	Some of the time	Most of the time	All of the time
PAUSE for thought or to let unseen characters speak?	Some of the time	Most of the time	All of the time
Vary PACE to express different emotions?	Some of the time	Most of the time	All of the time
Use appropriate MOVEMENT in the performance?	Some of the time	Most of the time	All of the time

KNOWLEDGE – 20 marks overall (conversation with the examiner)
L04 Know and understand the characters and situations in the chosen scenes.

Can your student discuss…	Pass	Merit	Distinction
The APPEARANCE of both characters?	Briefly	Securely	In detail
The FEELINGS of both characters during the scenes?	Briefly	Securely	In detail
The LOCATION of both scenes?	Briefly	Securely	In detail

Distinction: 80–100 • Merit 65–79 • Pass: 50–64

A learner fails if
- She scores 49 marks or less overall OR
- She scores 0 in one or more of the assessment criteria (L01, L02 etc)

FORMAT: SOLO EXAMS (15 MINUTES ALLOWED) AND DUOLOGUE EXAMS (20 MINUTES)
- 1 set scene from the *LAMDA Acting Anthology, Volume 3*
- 1 own-choice scene (between 2 and 3 minutes)
- Conversation

FORMAT: COMBINED EXAMS (25 MINUTES ALLOWED)
- 1 set duologue from the *LAMDA Acting Anthology, Volume 3*
- 2 own-choice solo scenes (between 2 and 3 minutes each)
- Conversation… OR
- 2 set solo scenes from the *LAMDA Acting Anthology, Volume 3*
- 1 own-choice duologue (between 2 and 3 minutes)
- Conversation

Scenes may be performed in any order.

Learners must announce the title, author and character of each scene before performing it. Decide on the phrasing and practise plenty of times:
- *For my set scene, I will be performing… by… I am playing the part of…*
- *My own-choice scene is… by… and I will be playing…*

Consider including a brief (one- or two-sentence) explanation of the context if your actors can manage it. It shows they have thought about their scene and adds polish to their performance. If an own-choice scene is not familiar to the examiner, the context will be useful.

Get students to test each other.
Recruit parents and siblings to help at home.
Explore different **line-learning** techniques.
Work on picking up **cues**.

Go through the glossary.

Walk around the room, varying speed according to the character's emotional energy (see page 25).
Look for high-tempo feelings (excitement, panic) and low-tempo feelings (sadness, exhaustion).

Insist on no peeking (see page 87).

Use **circle time** for conversation practice.

Sit at the back of the room during run-throughs.
Close your eyes during runs: can you hear the words?
Do regular **voice** exercises and **tongue-twisters**.

Look at **transitions** from one feeling or idea to the next.
Make sure each thought occupies its own space (see page 24).

Work on physical characterisation.
You read the words while the actor mimes the scene.
Do some **tableau** exercises.

During runs, freeze and do **thought tracking.**
Do abstract drawings or colour the script using **colours for feelings.**

Complete a character worksheet.
Complete other suggested art and writing tasks.
Do plenty of **hot seating.**

Complete a stage diagram.
Do a guided tour (see page 57).
Make a picture of the setting.

CHECKLIST: GRADE 1
Do you…
☐ know your lines?
☐ understand all of the words?
☐ project (a strong clear voice)?
☐ use pauses?
☐ vary the pace?
☐ move during the scene?
☐ stay in character?
Can you describe…
☐ your character's appearance?
☐ your character's feelings?
☐ the location of the scene?

*Words in **bold text** can be found in the index.*

Source Text

This scene has been adapted from Lewis Carroll's *Alice's Adventures in Wonderland,* Chapter VII. The events of the 'Mad Tea-Party' have been truncated and tweaked to create a short dramatic scene. The somewhat wordy original might appeal to a confident reader.

The stereotypical **Alice,** wide-eyed and rather conceited, is familiar. Stereotypes are ready-made performances, and many actors will automatically slip into them (by copying the voice and movements they have seen elsewhere). Instead, help your student to start afresh, investigate the text, and create her own Alice. The more choices she makes, the greater her sense of ownership. The performance will be richer and more heartfelt as a result.

> ### Project Work
> - CHARACTER WORKSHEET
> - KNOWLEDGE NOTES
> - STAGE DIAGRAM
> - RESEARCH: *Illustrations of the Mad Hatter's Tea Party*
> - ART: *Setting*
> - WRITING: *Full scene*
> - GLOSSARY
>
> | *populated* | *clearing* | *remark* |
> | *riddle* | *dormouse* | *raven* |

Reactions (Solo)

Alice has little patience with the absurdities and excesses of the world she finds herself in. She gives swift matter-of-fact responses to the weirdness of Wonderland. This scene is driven by Alice's reactions. Your actor must work hard to establish what the other characters are saying and doing through strong, clear reactions.

From when she first tries to sit down, Alice is involved in a three-way conversation with the Hare and the Hatter. Work with your actor on turning the solo scene into a group scene:

- Make a copy of the script on a large piece of paper with plenty of white space (use a smallish font with large line spacing).
- With your actor, find a moment where another character seems to have done or said something. What is Alice's reaction? What might the other character have said or done to prompt that response? Focus on what Alice is feeling at that moment (your actor will be asked about Alice's feelings in her LAMDA exam).
- Ask her to continue working through the script and add marks wherever someone else does or says something.
- Chop the script where she has made marks and lay the pieces out in order.
- With her, write stage directions or lines for the other characters onto pieces of paper and slot them into the gaps. Assign them to the Hare or the Hatter. (How are these two characters different?)
- Sellotape the script back together.
- Finally (as homework) ask her – with the help of her parents – to type up the full scene and bring copies for use in the next class. If this task is a stretch for her, do it yourself.

DEVELOPMENT (GROUP GAME): DON'T MAKE ME LAUGH

Matter-of-fact responses to absurd situations could provide the basis for a quick acting game:

- Use (or create with your students) two piles of cards: a pile of adjectives and a pile of nouns. A student takes one of each at random and mimes the result (for example, 'happy elephant'; 'crazy princess'; 'confused tree').
- Alice (or another player) commentates on what she is seeing matter-of-factly and without laughing.
- If she correctly guesses the mime, she (and the skilled mimer) win a point.

Reactions (Group)

Ask Alice and two classmates to play the whole scene. Encourage exaggerated performances from the other actors so that Alice has something to play off. Remind them to stage it in such a way that the audience can see Alice's face the whole time. The Hare's face and the Hatter's face need not be visible, as they won't be there in the final performance. Choose props to stand in for the Dormouse and the teapot.

- As the actors run the scene, encourage strong reactions from Alice and keep focusing on her feelings about what is happening.
- Try asking her to react with her face first and her words afterwards.
- Move the other actors off the stage and replay the scene. They speak their lines from off stage. Alice plays to them as if they are in position.
- Repeat the exercise. This time the other two actors whisper their lines.
- Repeat – they speak their lines in their heads and clap when they have finished. Alice reacts on the clap. Get her used to the feel of the gaps. Encourage her to 'hear' the lines spoken by the other characters in her head (but make sure that she doesn't mouth them).
- If she speeds up when performing solo, repeat the stage with the claps.

Setting

Ask Alice to find every bit of information the text provides about what the setting looks like: the clearing in the woods, the Hatter's house, the table under the tree, and so on. How does she imagine extra details? What is the weather like? What is the house made of? How big is the table? She can draw the setting in some quiet time in class or at home. Discuss her drawing. How would she feel about this place if she saw it for the first time?

Alternatively, search for illustrations (in books or online) or film stills of the Mad Hatter's Tea Party. How closely do these depictions match her own mental image of the scene?

> ❋ **FACIAL EXPRESSIONS** ❋
>
> Include grinning, gurning and grimacing in your warm-up for every lesson so that your actors lose their inhibitions when it comes to using facial expressions to show feelings. It is impossible to be disgusted, shocked or ecstatic with a poker face. Join in when asking your youngsters to puff out their cheeks, stick out their tongues and blow raspberries. Chewing magical gum (which changes flavour or grows in size) will exercise every muscle in their face.

THE NECKLACE OF FINGERS

by Jill O'Hare ❋ *Acting Anthology page 12*

It's Fun to Frighten

In his own words, **Angulimala** is 'nasty and cruel'. He kills people so that he can collect their fingers for his necklace. He has nearly reached his goal of a thousand fingers, and he is extremely proud of this achievement. He is feared by everyone in the kingdom and takes delight in the fear he spreads.

Your actor must repeat this pattern: do something frightening – see the fear it creates – feel proud. This scene is played to an audience; whenever Angulimala sees the fear on their faces, he is joyous.

Most children (certainly those who have been on a rollercoaster or a ghost train) will be familiar with the association between fear and laughter. Most will have made someone jump by leaping out and shouting 'boo!' Ask them why that's fun. (Perhaps it's because the ambusher feel scary or powerful – that's how Angulimala feels.)

Here's a game that will connect the actor with the blend of feelings Angulimala expresses:

TMATTY (TELL ME ABOUT THE TIME THAT YOU...)

In this exercise, you invent a past event or achievement in your student's life. You say 'Robert, tell me about the time that you...' Without any forethought, Robert recounts it. For this scene, prepare some events with suitably cruel or gruesome twists. (Take account of squeamishness and sensitivities and decide what limits of tastefulness you wish to stay within.) Remind players how proud they are of what they have done. Encourage them to show off as they tell you about the time that they ate a worm, stole their teacher's bicycle, chopped their own hand off or created the world's worst stink. They must speak for thirty seconds (or a minute) without stopping, except to laugh – laughter is definitely allowed.

Now ask your Angulimala actor to tell you about the time he collected forty fingers in one go (remind him that he killed forty of the king's men by making their horses dizzy). Ideally, do this early in rehearsals, before he has learnt his lines. He can improvise his account. Ask him to take the stage and tell you again, re-enacting the events as he describes them. Encourage him to be a show-off. Finally he can play the text with the same glee and pride.

Movement: Leap and Pounce

This scene offers an opportunity for strong physical characterisation. First check that your actor has understood Angulimala's lifestyle. What is a brigand? (Someone who ambushes and robs people.) How would Angulimala need to move around in order to succeed? Does he work alone or as part of a gang?

Project Work

- CHARACTER WORKSHEET
- KNOWLEDGE NOTES
- STAGE DIAGRAM
- RESEARCH: *Animal movement*
- OUTING: *Zoo trip*
- ART: *Setting; necklace of fingers*

GLOSSARY

victim	catastrophe	lair
deed	plague	pounce
unsuspecting	vow	crouch
glower	threatening	menacingly
brigand	lead a merry dance	

8

❉ WORKING SAFELY ONLINE ❉

*Y*ou will find suggestions for online research tasks throughout this book. There is so much useful work your students can do online when preparing a performance. However, youngsters should never work online unsupervised. An innocent search request may throw upsetting and threatening images and videos onto the screen. You need to safeguard your students with the same diligence as if you were taking them on a trip to a busy city centre.

If you are setting an online research task to be done in class, get students to work in pairs or groups, using only a computer that you have full control over. Keep an eye on them as they work.

Install a browser (Safari, Chrome, etc) exclusively for use by your students so that they can bookmark pages and access search history without interfering with your own online work. Try search engines aimed specifically at children, such as safesearchkids.com and kidzsearch.com. The filters on these sites are very strict, and some acceptable material does not make it through. If you have a Google account, you can set up custom safety filters on Google and YouTube so that the net is widened a little. If you know what the research task will be, do the search yourself beforehand and save the results (if you're happy with them) for students to look at in class.

Whatever practices you adopt, set them down in an internet safety policy document and give copies to parents. Ask them to implement the same procedures at home when your students are conducting online research for homework you have set them.

Find all the words in the scene that describe Angulimala's movements: he leaps, spins, crouches, climbs and pounces. We also know that he is strong and can run fast. If he were an animal, what animal would he be? A leopard? A monkey? A squirrel? When the actor has chosen, he can research the way his animal moves by looking for videos online (any online research should be closely monitored: see the box above) or even with a trip to the zoo. When he has some ideas, ask him to move around the playing space as if he were the animal he has chosen (upright rather than on all-fours). Can he play the scene in full animal mode? If not, how and where might he include some animal movement?

Setting

Angulimala's physicality will also be affected by his surroundings. The scene is set in rural northern India; Kosala was in modern-day Uttar Pradesh. Look at photos (in books or online) for ideas about what Angulimala's road, lair and hiding place might look like. Draw a picture of Angulimala in hiding, ready to pounce.

Other Ideas: Prop Making

Although LAMDA's exam regulations prohibit full costume and stipulate that props are to be kept to a minimum, it would be fun to make a necklace of fingers. Plasticine, playdough and even carrots might be made to look like severed fingers and threaded onto a shoelace. Plenty of online video tutorials suggest ways of creating home-made special effects (FX) for stage and film (check all videos for suitability). You could use your necklace in rehearsals only or, if it doesn't impede the performance, during the exam as well.

Character

You and your actor have the freedom to create many of the details of **Molly**'s life, as well as the circumstances of this scene. Work together to create a back story.

First mine the text for all the information the writer has chosen to give you about Molly:

- She hates piano lessons and piano practice.
- Her lessons are 'stupid' and she has to play 'dumb little pieces'.
- She finds playing the piano really difficult, especially keeping time; even after a year she can only play basic pieces with one hand.
- In her opinion, her piano teacher is old, big, yells when Molly makes a mistake and has a house that is freezing in winter.
- In her opinion, her mother doesn't listen to her; nobody listens to children.
- Her mother will not let her give up the piano because she has talent.

This information should start to give your actor a feel for Molly, and after reading through the scene a few times, she might be able to 'hear' Molly's voice. Now you can start filling in the gaps in your picture of the character.

The process of creating a character involves making choices. You guide the process by asking the right questions, but let your actor give the answers. Give her as much creative control as you can. The more decisions she makes, the more she will own her character, and her performance will be richer and more truthful as a result. (The least helpful thing you can do is to give line readings – 'say it like this'). Decisions should be strong – outlaw the word 'quite'. There are many ways in which you can set about creating a character:

Project Work

- **CHARACTER WORKSHEET**
- **KNOWLEDGE NOTES**
- **STAGE DIAGRAM**
- **OBSERVATION:** *Playing the piano*
- **ART:** *Mrs Campbell; Mrs C's house/ living room; Molly; M's bedroom; the ideal Wednesday afternoon*
- **WRITING:** *Story about Molly; Molly's diary; letter to Mrs Campbell*

GLOSSARY

grand piano	*awkward*
impersonate	*talent*

✳ HOT SEATING (1) ✳

*P*utting an actor in the 'hot seat' is a great way of delving into the background of a scene and the back story of a character. The actor takes the stage and gives instinctive answers to questions posed by the teacher. The actor is in character and answers in the first person.

Remind your actor that there are no right or wrong answers and that neither of you knows the answers beforehand. It is a process of discovery: take the pressure off. Allow her a few seconds before answering if she needs it, but try to get her to work off the cuff. Don't worry if answers clash with the text. Keep the exercise going – you can iron out any discrepancies afterwards.

The actor can embody the character's voice and physicality to whatever degree he or she feels able. The important thing is to try to think as the character thinks. The answers might be different from those she would give in real life! For more thoughts on hot seating, see page 113.

- Through straightforward discussion. You might start with character details before going on to investigate the circumstances of the scene:
  - How old is Molly?
  - Who lives at home with her?
  - Who is her best friend?
  - What does she like to wear? What does she like to eat?
  - What exactly does she wish she were doing on a Wednesday afternoon?
  - Where is Molly? What is she doing? Who is she talking to?
  - Why does she start talking about her piano lessons?
- Through hot-seating (see box opposite).
- By drawing and making. Your student might draw:
  - Mrs Campbell
  - Molly
  - Molly's bedroom
  - Molly's ideal Wednesday afternoon.
- By writing. Your student might write:
  - A brief story about Molly in the third person
  - A page from Molly's diary
  - A letter to Mrs Campbell apologising for making mistakes.

Remember with these drawing and writing exercises that the process – the thinking that goes on while your student is doing it – matters more than the results. See the box on page 44.

Setting

Mrs Campbell's house is not well heated. Lessons take place at a grand piano in the living room (so the room must be large), with Mrs Campbell sitting next to Molly on the piano bench. Your actor can imagine all the other details. Does she know someone with a piano? With a large draughty house? Is there a music room at school? She could take photos of places that have similar features to the scene's location. Alternatively, she can imagine the setting entirely. Fix details through drawing or a guided tour (see page 57).

Voice

There are a few potential tongue-twisters in this scene. Remind your actor that projecting her voice depends as much on clarity as it does on volume. In a a small space, clarity is more important than volume. Good diction – speaking the consonants clearly – is the key factor. Many young actors, with their gappy teeth and squishy tongues, need regular practice at diction. Find the tongue-twisters in this (or any) scene and drill them.

- *She has a great big grand piano*
- *Mrs Campbell counts out loud*
- *She says I have talent*

It's a good idea to practise these as part of a general voice warm-up. For variety, try intoning or singing them. For a group, take tongue-twisting phrases from everyone's scenes. For advice on using tongue-twisters in your class, see page 21. More thoughts on warming up the voice can be found on page 91.

Cyclone

In a group, **Dorothy**'s classmates can be the cyclone. They form a circle around Dorothy and walk (or skip or jog) around her. They make wind and storm noises, which increase in volume and intensity as Dorothy works through the scene. She tries to speak clearly above the noise. At the end, everyone crashes to the ground in a heap before Dorothy gets up to see where she has landed. For added fun, shout out where the house has landed each time; students immediately have to mime being there (the moon; fairyland; a zombie uprising.)

Give Dorothy practice at 'seeing' the various items caught up in the cyclone. Nominate students to be the chicken coop, old lady, cow, rowing boat and so on. To help Dorothy identify which item is which, she can draw pictures for her classmates to hold up. Before referencing each item, Dorothy locates it in the whirl and stays focused on it as it spins in the cyclone.

Can Dorothy evoke the cyclone when she does the scene on her own?

Solo Version

In a solo class, you might have to play the items whirling in the storm. Every time Dorothy sees a new item, she must locate you and stay focused on you. Alternatively, draw pictures and stick them onto the wall.

Follow-up

Consolidate with a drawing of the house spinning in the cyclone amid all the flying objects. An online image search for Kansas farmhouses will give ideas about Dorothy's home (see page 9 for notes on working online). You could look at stills from the film. Discourage your actor from watching the film; her own Dorothy is preferable to a copy of Judy Garland's.

Variations on Fear

Having established the high energy required for the scene, work on finding variety, so that it is not all delivered in a rush and on one note. How would your student feel if she were whisked up in a cyclone? Has she had a thrilling and terrifying experience – on a rollercoaster, a trampoline, or a water slide? See if she can find five or six different responses. These might include frightened, terrified, excited, panicking, amazed, dizzy and so on.

Help Dorothy to decide where she experiences these different emotions. Lay out a pile of highlighters or felt-tips and ask her to choose a colour for each feeling. Decide where each feeling belongs and add colours or highlights to the script. Dorothy can also colour-code her picture of the house or the pictures of the whirling items. Do a run of the scene in which she says the feeling word before speaking the section of text it applies to.

Project Work

- CHARACTER WORKSHEET
- KNOWLEDGE NOTES
- STAGE DIAGRAM
- RESEARCH: *Kansas farm*
- ART: *Whirling items; Dorothy's house in the cyclone*

GLOSSARY

Kansas	storm shelter	coop
cyclone	debris	duck
whirl	swirl	twirl

✴ LOSING GAMES AND GOING OUT ✴

*T*here is nothing like a competitive game to inject some energy into a class of youngsters. Even the sleepiest end-of-Friday-afternoon session will burst into life at the thought that there are going to be winners. If you offer a prize or reward for the winner (even something as humble as a sticker or a pencil), the level of engagement in the exercise will shoot up.

Unfortunately every competition has its losers as well as its winners. Losing games is a fact of life that some children struggle with. It can be heartbreaking. Yet competition is everywhere all of the time, and learning to cope with defeat is an extremely valuable life skill to teach a child.

Find ways of lessening the pain of losing a game (or going out) by making losing less serious. Give losers the opportunity to do something silly, such as going to sit on a whoopee cushion or wearing a silly wig for sixty seconds. Alternatively, have a losing catchphrase, such as 'silly me!' or 'doesn't matter!' Congratulate and reward the winners and then focus the losers (lightehartedly) on the glory that awaits them next time or the revenge that will one day be theirs. Comfort losers with the thought that surely it will be their turn to win next time.

Themed Games

Involve the whole group in work on this scene with some themed games:

- SQUIRT! (AN OZ-THEMED VARIATION ON SPLAT!)
  Students standing in a circle are wicked witches. Dorothy stands centre with a water pistol (her fingers) and shouts 'SQUIRT!' as she fires it at a witch. That witch ducks, and witches to either side race to shoot each other over her head (also by pointing fingers and shouting 'SQUIRT!'). One of the three has been shot; she screams 'I'm melting!!' as she disintegrates into a puddle. For the final duel, the two surviving witches stand back to back. As Dorothy slowly counts, they take a step away from each other. When Dorothy shouts 'SQUIRT!' instead of the next number, they turn and squirt each other. Fastest squirter wins; the loser melts.

- STORM SOUNDSCAPE
  You start a regular sound, and one by one around the circle, your students follow until everyone is making the same sound. Then you make a new sound. Students continue with the first sound until their turn comes again; at that point they move onto the next sound. The storm builds to a crashing crescendo before dying back down. Here's the order:

  1. Rub hands (the wind builds)
  2. Click fingers (raindrops)
  3. Clap hands (rain gets heavy)
  4. Slap thighs (downpour)
  5. Stomp feet (deluge)
  6. Slap thighs
  7. Clap hands
  8. Click fingers
  9. Rub hands
  10. Silence.

- TREE IN THE CYCLONE (AN OZ-THEMED CIRCLE OF TRUST)
  Students form a tight circle around Dorothy. She crosses her arms over her chest and stands rigid, like a tree. Students in the circle put both hands in front of them, elbows bent, palms facing and almost touching Dorothy. Staying rooted (and resisting the urge to step), she tips backwards into the hands. Students gently push her around the circle in all directions. Ask Dorothy to close her eyes. Students can make gentle wind noises.

Setting and Staging

The writer has not specified a location, so your actor should make a choice. Guide her towards the final sentences, which show that **Margie** must be outdoors. Your actor should also be able to deduce the time of year (February). Ask further questions as you build up a picture of the location. Encourage your actor to use her imagination by assuring her that there are no right and wrong answers. The more decisions she makes, the more ownership she will have of her performance:

> ### Project Work
> - CHARACTER WORKSHEET
> - KNOWLEDGE NOTES
> - STAGE DIAGRAM
> - RESEARCH: *Celebrities/idols*
> - ART: *Marcus; classmates; the Valentine's card*
> - WRITING: *Poem for Marcus*
> - GLOSSARY
>
> crush   keepsake   Jammie Dodger

- Are you in school or somewhere else?
- Where exactly are you? Are you sitting? What can you see around you?
- What time of day is it? What's the weather like?
- Are you allowed to be eating those sweets?

Margie's best friend is close by, but Margie's focus is frequently drawn to Marcus, who is some distance away. If you place Marcus out front somewhere, the audience will see Margie's facial expressions.

OTHER CHARACTERS

During rehearsal, it will help Margie to have someone on stage with her playing her friend – especially when it comes to working out the business with the sweets. You could use real sweets – it will be easier for your actor to have an attitude to the precious gift – but only if they can be eaten quickly and easily and won't interfere with Margie's delivery.

Marcus takes a lot of Margie's focus, so it might help your actor to have a stand-in for him, too. You could find moments where the two catch each other's eye. Is Margie pleased or embarrassed?

However, a Marcus stand-in is not vital, and a real Marcus might bring out the yuck factor or the giggle factor of romantic subject matter. You could keep the kind, straight-teethed, curly-haired boy imaginary so that Margie can create exactly the Marcus she wants. Ask her to bring in some magazines aimed at her age group that include film stars, pop stars or other idols. Look for boxed profiles of celebrities and ask her to create one for Marcus.

Margie can keep any Marcus research secret from the class, and even from you. The feeling that she has something precious and private will connect her with her character and might sharpen her performance.

Roses Are Red

For homework or quiet time, Margie can make the Valentine's card. She could also draw Jacqueline Mason, Ian Turton and Samantha Fellows. She (with her stand-in) should create a back story for the friend she is talking to.

Group Games: Keeping a Secret

Secrets are powerful – challenging to keep and thrilling to share. To help your Margie actor engage with these feelings – and to give the whole class a chance to have fun and be ingenious – play some games involving secrets:

- **DON'T TELL ANYONE!**

  A playground-gossip version of the classic whispering game. Make a wide circle. Margie runs to the next person and whispers in her ear, 'Marcus sat next to me at lunch' (or similar). The second student runs to the third and whispers 'Marcus sat next to her at lunch'. Each person whispers only once. If a student can't hear what has been whispered, she must make what sense of it she can. Continue until the last student swaggers up to Margie and taunts her: 'Marcus sat next to you at lunch!' – or whatever garbled version of the secret has made it around the circle. Play again, with others inventing secrets to start the game off.

- **LOOK INTO MY EYES**

  Two teams face each other across a long table. Team A has a coin. Players pass it backwards and forwards under the table until the player on Team B says 'Look Into My Eyes.' Team A players close both fists tight and place them on the table in front of them. They look into the opposing player's eyes. Can he or she guess just from their faces which fist holds the coin?

- **SCHOOL TRIP**

  Tell your class 'I am going on a school trip and I am bringing sandwiches.' Prompt the next student to take her turn. She makes a different offer: 'I am going on a school trip and I am bringing crisps.' Politely tell her she can't come. Keep going; sooner or later, someone will make a correct offer (perhaps by accident). Tell him he can come but mustn't give the secret away. Students will be intrigued and desperate to join the trip. The trick is simple – the item proposed must begin with the same letter as the student's name. Steven takes sandwiches, Rafael takes Ribena, and so on.

- **WHOOPS JOHNNY!**

  Show your students a sequence. The words are 'Johnny, Johnny, Johnny, Johnny, Whoops Johnny, Whoops Johnny, Johnny, Johnny, Johnny.' Hold up one hand, fingers spread. With the index finger of your other hand, touch each finger in turn, starting with your little finger. Say 'Johnny' each time you touch a finger. After you have touched your index finger, slide down and up to the tip of your thumb, then back the other way to the tip of your index finger. Each slide is accompanied by 'Whoops' and then 'Johnny' as you land. Three more 'Johnnies' take you back to where you started. Your students must copy your sequence exactly. What most of them will miss is the way you folded your arms after you finished. That is part of the sequence, and until they include it, they are getting it wrong.

More concentration games are on the web page which accompanies this book.

When playing the games, let Margie in on the secret. Ask her (and others) afterwards how it feels to have a secret. Focus on what happens to the face and body when they answer the question. Holding a secret inside creates tension. They may look gleeful or suspicious. It may be obvious that they are hiding something. Margie can use the same physicality when playing her scene.

Scruffy on Trial

Your actor will need to unpick the story of Scruffy from **Sam**'s recollections. You can turn this background exploration into a fun exercise involving the whole class.

Ask Sam to read through the scene while the class listens. Check their understanding of the situation by asking a few questions along the way. Sam says whether their answers are right or wrong. At the end, ask the group what they think has become of Scruffy. Sam chooses the outcome that feels right to him.

Introduce a soft-toy dog to the class. This is a guest actor who is going to play the part of Scruffy. Give it a 'real' name and show that it is very excited (or nervous) to be cast as Scruffy. Discuss its suitability for the role of Scruffy. Does it look right? What does the text reveal about Scruffy's appearance? Does anyone know what Labradors and Irish Setters look like? (You could do some on-the-spot research or set this as a homework task.) What do we know about Scruffy's personality? Will your toy convince in the role?

You are going to put Scruffy on trial. Decide what he is charged with (e.g. gross misconduct; disgusting behaviour; theft). Divide your class into two groups. One group, led by Sam, will be the defence, and the other, led by Sam's Mum, will be the prosecution.

The prosecution should write a list of at least five events condemning Scruffy. These can be taken straight from the text with a few invented ones added. The defence must write a list of five or more positive contributions Scruffy makes to life. Sam can take the lead in inventing these.

Stage the trial, with Scruffy in the witness box and you as judge. Ask Sam to present his case in Scruffy's defence. Depending on time, Sam can just read his list or speak at more length. You could cross-examine Sam or call other members of the defence as witnesses – a next-door neighbour, an old lady Scruffy helped across the road, etc. Mum presents the case for the prosecution in the same way. Whoever is playing her should remember how appalled she is by Scruffy. When both sides have had their say, you present your judgement. However convinced you are by the defence, Scruffy is guilty as charged.

Finally, hand over the decision on sentencing to the prosecution. Mum must condemn Scruffy to the fate the group (led by Sam) agreed on during the initial discussion – be it death by hanging or banishment to the pet shop. The punishment can be outlandish; in the scene Sam does not know what has happened to Scruffy, so he may be imagining the worst.

Project Work

- CHARACTER WORKSHEET
- KNOWLEDGE NOTES
- STAGE DIAGRAM
- RESEARCH: Labrador/Irish Setter
- ART: Scruffy
- WRITING: Scruffy timeline; newspaper front page

GLOSSARY

scruffy	joint	bossed
mongrel	munch	impatient
fleas	hysterical	fit
Labrador	ultimatum	froth
Irish Setter	act on impulse	

FOLLOW-UPS

Depending on how immersed he has been in the exercise, your Sam actor might feel sad and aggrieved at the outcome. Point out that this is exactly how Sam feels and ask him to remember the feeling of dejection.

Ask the defence to spell out again – so Sam is clear – Scruffy's list of offences. As homework or during quiet time, Sam should create a timeline. If the incident with the roast chicken happened last Sunday, Dad took three days to think about the ultimatum and yesterday Scruffy was frothing at the mouth, today is Friday. How long has Scruffy has been with Sam's family?

All this focus on Scruffy should give Sam plenty of ideas when it comes to making a portrait of his dog. As well as Scruffy itself, his picture could include fleas, apple crumble and all the other misdeeds. A cookery magazine and a dog magazine should provide plenty of good photos for a collage.

Another good quiet-time task would be to create a newspaper front page reporting on Scruffy's verdict and sentence.

SOLO VERSION

You can stage the trial in a solo class; it is an excellent way of getting a clear picture of Scruffy's misdemeanours. Sam can play both prosecution and defence. Playing the prosecution will give him an opportunity to work on a Mum character. He can prepare his arguments as homework before the class.

Mum

Sam is angry with his Mum, so his impersonation of her is likely to exaggerate qualities he doesn't like (bossiness, prudishness, hysteria and so on). Encourage Sam to lampoon her. The trial may have provided a Mum he can base his caricature on. If so, you could continue to use the Mum actor in rehearsal. She can speak Mum's lines in a couple of rehearsals or run-throughs. You can also use her in improvisations.

Improvisations

Engage your actor with Sam's situation by improvising episodes described or hinted at in the scene. Here are some possible scenes to improvise:

- Sam brings Scruffy home for the first time.
- Mum discovers Scruffy on Sam's bed.
- Dinner last Sunday.
- Mum and Dad discuss Scruffy.

Improvising can be nerve-wracking, so take the pressure off. Reassure students that, since you are not giving them much time to prepare, you know that their improvised scenes might be rough. Check that improvisers know their character, the situation and what their character wants. For example, in the first scene suggested above:

- Sam wants to make Mum like Scruffy.
- Mum wants to keep the house clean as she has guests coming round.
- They both want to avoid an argument if possible.

If your actors are clear about what they want, some drama should follow. For more notes on improvising with youngsters, see page 29, and for more on wants and obstacles, see page 116.

In A Dark, Dark Wood

Hansel must create his surroundings and establish the spooky atmosphere. This themed visualisation exercise will help set the tone.

The exercise can be scary for youngsters. Warn your class that you are all going to go on a make-believe spooky adventure in a dark wood. At the end there will be a witch, and they must all scream and run to the other side of the room. The witch has very sensitive ears, and if they scream very loudly she will vanish. You could play the witch yourself and die dramatically.

First they walk happily around the space. It's daytime, and they are in a pretty wood. They spot birds and butterflies and pick flowers. They have just eaten a picnic and have a pleasantly full tummy. Commentate until they are immersed and responding silently to your cues. Suddenly they feel tired and decide to have a nap. Let them lie down and close their eyes for a little while.

They stretch and open their eyes. Now it is night time. Their bodies ache all over. It is silent and dark. Was that an animal scurrying away, or just the leaves rustling? They are very hungry. They think they can make out a path and walk slowly towards it. Now use a quiet voice to build tension:

In a dark, dark wood there were some dark, dark trees
By the dark, dark trees there were some dark, dark plants
Under the dark, dark plants there was a dark, dark path
Along the dark, dark path there was a dark, dark clearing
In the dark, dark clearing there was a dark, dark house
In the dark, dark house there was a dark, dark door
By the dark, dark door there was a dark, dark window
In the dark, dark window there was a… nice old lady
But the nice old lady was a… WITCH!

Project Work

- CHARACTER WORKSHEET
- KNOWLEDGE NOTES
- STAGE DIAGRAM
- RESEARCH: *Hansel and Gretel*
- OBSERVATION: *Walking at night; feeling hungry*
- OUTING: *Forest*
- ART: *The old lady; the gingerbread house*

GLOSSARY

gingerbread	tentatively	marzipan
ache	abruptly	treacle
rustle	liquorice	cottage

FOLLOW-UP

Give everyone a moment to calm down before talking through the experience. Focus on Hansel, since his body language is key to his performance. Discuss the differences between walking through the wood during the daytime and at night. How about the differences between walking around when happy and when scared? Full and hungry? Relaxed and aching? Use the discussion to help Hansel to make decisions about physicality – how quickly will he move? How will he place his feet on the ground? Where will he be looking? He says he is not afraid. Is this true? Is it cold in the wood?

Hansel can also do some self-observation for homework. Ask him to notice when he is feeling hungry (first thing in the morning or in the middle of the afternoon). Before eating or drinking, can he spend five minutes just being hungry? How does being hungry affect his mood? What happens in his body? Does he think or speak differently?

If the days are short, ask him also to find an opportunity to go for a walk in the dark. Can he get an adult to accompany him to a park or garden? How does he move in strange surroundings when it is difficult to see?

Night and Day
Several scenes in the anthology are set at night, so it might be worth practising nocturnal movement with the whole group:
- Students moves around the room as though in a pretty wood in daytime. At your signal (a clap or a tambourine) it is suddenly dark and silent. Switch back and forth.
- Students in turn move across the playing space, and classmates – who have drawn quick pictures of a sun on one piece of paper and a moon on another – guess whether it is day or night by holding up the right picture.

Guess the Smell
Before playing this game, find out about any allergies your students have.

A sudden change of mood, rhythm and pace is triggered first by what Hansel smells and then by what he sees. A game of Guess the Smell pulls the same sensory triggers. Blindfold Hansel, sit him at the table and place various pungent substances in front of him. He tries to identify each one before you remove his blindfold. Focus him on how it feels to smell something familiar (or unfamiliar) and on his reaction when the blindfold is removed.

The smells should not be foul – no blue cheese or old socks. Hansel likes what he is smelling. You could use cinnamon, popcorn and baby wipes.

In a group, everyone can have a turn. Remember to focus Hansel's attention on his classmates' facial expressions during the game.

Further Ideas
- In rehearsal, have a stand-in for Gretel. Make sure Hansel really observes and addresses his little sister when he speaks to her.
- Map out Hansel's journey to the house. If the old lady is placed out front, his reaction when he sees her will be shared with the audience.
- Many young actors struggle to convince when miming eating. Give plenty of practice – and see the box on page 104 for some thoughts on mime.
- Draw the old lady.
- Draw the gingerbread house. Alternatively, make a model from craft materials or even an edible model; look for instructions online.
- As an end-of-class treat, tell the whole story of Hansel and Gretel. You could break it into five-minute installments. You can download a text from the web page which accompanies this book. Don't read the story; learn the key events in order and tell it your own way, making plenty of eye contact with your students. The story will be much more vivid as a result.

What Does Badger Want?

This scene is driven by **Badger**'s determination to 'convert' or 'rescue' Toad. He wants to persuade Ratty and Mole to join him in this mission. For the scene to have dramatic interest, the outcome should be in the balance. Badger might fail: he might not persuade Ratty and Mole. The plan might not be sound. They might not get to Toad in time… add jeopardy wherever you can.

If you have a class, use stand-ins for Ratty and Mole. Ask them to be doubtful about what Badger is saying and reluctant to join forces with him, so that he must fight hard to rally them to his cause. They will only join him at the end if his words inspire them.

Project Work

- CHARACTER WORKSHEET
- KNOWLEDGE NOTES
- STAGE DIAGRAM
- RESEARCH: Badgers
- ART: Toad going for a drive; Ratty, Mole and Badger in Ratty's riverbank home
- WRITING: Letter to Toad demanding he stop his crazy behaviour

GLOSSARY

caravan	trustworthy	comparatively
escapade	source	decent-minded
outline	approval or return	fit
convert	array	up and doing
formal	singularly	ere
take in hand	hideous	accompany
back up	habiliments	instantly
sound	dear to	accomplish

Mr Toad

Your actor will need a clear picture of Toad's madcap and irresponsible behaviour. Watching video clips would be an enjoyable way into the world of the story. The entertaining Thames Television series (1984–1990) is one of many adaptations available on DVD. You might be able to find clips online. At the time of writing, a YouTube search for 'The Wind in the Willows: Toad's Motorcar' returns an excellent montage from the 1980s TV series.

You might also work with the source text (a 1908 children's classic by Kenneth Grahame). Chapter 4 offers a good way into the characters of Ratty, Mole and Badger and includes a vivid account of Toad's excesses.

Source

The scene itself is adapted from the first paragraphs of Chapter 6 of *The Wind in the Willows*. Read to your student (who listens rather than reading along). Or ask your student to highlight everything Badger says, then read together, with your student playing Badger and you as narrator and the other characters. In a group, other students can play Ratty and Mole. With a larger group, you can include Otter and the two little hedgehogs, who appear later in the chapter. The tableau exercise on page 56 would work well with this text.

When Badger catches up with Toad, he gives him a dressing-down. Badger's words make it clear why he is so concerned about the way his friend is carrying on. Despite all the warnings he's been given, Toad's reckless behaviour is getting him into trouble with the police and is 'getting us animals a bad name in the district.' Discuss what might be the consequences for Badger, Mole and Ratty if Toad is allowed to continue.

❊ TONGUE TWISTERS (1) ❊

Saying tongue-twisters is a vital drama exercise at any age and at any level. They warm up the speaking muscles and give young actors a chance to practise tricky consonants:

Sly Sam slurps Sally's soup   *Six slimy snails sailed silently*

These phrases (and many hundreds more) can be used as drills in class or – since they are easily memorable – taken home for practice. The best ones have sensual or sensory appeal. Young actors relish twisting their tongues around phrases that are slippery, slithery and squelchy.

You could choose (or invent) tongue-twisters that are relevant to the scene you are working on:

It's high time that Toad toed the line   *Badger jabbed a jagged badge*

Ask students to come up with alliterative or rhyming tongue-twisters based on their own name:

Jack jumped into juicy jelly   *Silly Lily felt chilly*

Clear diction is more difficult for youngsters than it is for adults. You may have students for whom English is not a first language or not the only language. So make tongue-twisting playful. Ensure that there is no shame in getting tripped up.

Tell your young actors that the tongue-twister is a clever enemy. It is trying to force them to make a mistake. The only way of defeating the tongue-twister is to attack back. Engage the muscles of the mouth, say it slowly and strongly, and victory will be yours.

If the book does not appeal to your student, suggest that he listen to an audiobook. A good recording, narrated by Bernard Cribbins, is available on the BBC Learning School Radio website, which also provides resources for teachers (there is a link on the web page which accompanies this book).

Diction

The role of Badger is a vocally challenging one for a young actor, and you will need to work on diction. Ask your student to read the scene slowly aloud. Where are the phrases that are trying to trip him up?

- *[an] exceptionally powerful motor car*
- *singularly hideous habiliments*
- *accompany me instantly to Toad Hall*

To speak these phrases clearly, your actor will have to engage his speaking muscles. Warm them up (see page 91); any exercise that stretches cheeks, lips and tongue will be beneficial, so pull faces or chew invisible gum (see page 7).

Now ask your actor to exaggerate his mouth movements while speaking Badger's tricky phrases. You should hear them perfectly with your eyes closed. In performance, make sure your actor applies conscious effort when speaking the phrases. Make this effort an acting choice:

- Badger is someone who speaks clearly all the time.
- Badger is speaking emphatically to keep his audience's attention.
- Badger is slightly deaf.
- There is background noise.

Further Ideas

- Draw any of the characters and situations you have explored.
- Work on Badger's physicality (eg, large paws, solid build and snuffling).
- Write a letter to Toad. Detail his irresponsible behaviour and insist he stop.

Poor Tom

Tom's situation is dire. On a lovely Saturday morning he should be taking it easy, yet he finds himself having to whitewash a fence. To make matters worse, all his friends will pass by as they head to the river to swim or fish.

A game will bring Tom's situation to life. Come up with some ordinary activities, then imagine who would enjoy each activity and who would hate it:

- ballet dancing – a ballerina / The Incredible Hulk
- tidying up Lego – a domestic robot / a messy child
- eating carrots – a rabbit / a dog
- painting a fence – a keen fence painter / Tom Sawyer.

Project Work

- CHARACTER WORKSHEET
- KNOWLEDGE NOTES
- STAGE DIAGRAM
- RESEARCH: Missouri
- OBSERVATION: Doing something you don't want to do
- ART: Saturday morning fishing
- WRITING: The Plan; dialogue with Ben

GLOSSARY

sheer genius	it would hardly do	
whitewash	trash	pushover
grumble	particular	newly
foot/yard	fixed	acquired
laughing stock	tackle	
trade	barrel	

Tom finds a space in the room and mimes one of the activities. First he imagines that he really loves what he is doing. On your cue, he switches to loathing it. There should be a strong contrast between enthusiastic engagement in the task and deep dislike of it.

After trying a few activities, discuss what happens in the body when you are forced to do something that you don't want to do.

DEVELOPMENT

When it comes to painting the fence, deepen the misery: Tom stares at the unpainted fence and imagines what he would love to be doing instead on this Saturday morning. Ask him to describe the imagined scene to you in vivid detail – can he transport himself into that bliss? Now come back to the fence and ask him to pick up the brush. How does it feel in his hand? How does the fence look? What is the feeling in his legs?

Work on Tom's attitude during the moment near the top of the scene when he picks up the brush and puts it down again.

For homework or during quiet time, Tom can draw an idyllic picture of himself fishing from a sunny riverbank.

Scheming

Tom's inventiveness drives this scene. If you have a class (and before everyone knows the scene), hand out copies of the text that stop at 'I'll pretend not to have seen him.' Ask Tom to read up to that point, then ask classmates to come up with ideas about what Tom's plan might be. Reveal that the scene ends with Tom sitting on a barrel, munching Ben's apple and watching Ben happily paint the fence. How does everyone imagine that Tom has achieved that?

Tom can observe his classmates as they hatch their plans. What happens to the eyes, face and body when we come up with a brilliant idea? Can Tom incorporate the same body language in his own performance? Practise the section that begins with him emptying his pockets.

Finish up by reading the missing portion of the scene. Tom can explain to the group what his plan was. Share Tom's conclusion: to get someone to want something, all you have to do is 'make the thing difficult to attain.'

FOLLOW-UP

A publisher has offered to pay Tom a hundred pounds for the right to print Tom's plan in a book. Tom must write his plan down as a list of instructions.

Bet You're Jealous!

Tom's game is to make the whitewashing of the fence seem very special. Ben becomes so jealous that not only does he wants to whitewash the fence himself, but he 'pays' Tom for the privilege with an apple. Turn this dramatic element of the story into a game:

- Come up with some mundane tasks – peeling potatoes, counting marbles, threading needles, and so on.
- Tom finds a space and takes up the task without enthusiasm.
- At your signal, he must suddenly makes the task seem extremely special. Play along as Ben. At first you think the task looks boring or arduous. Can Tom change your mind and make it seem fascinating?
- In a class, make the game competitive: students find a space in the room and carry out a mundane task. Which one looks the most intriguing? How did the winner succeed?
- Round off by returning to the text of the scene and putting all of these observations into practice. Start with 'Wait a moment! I've got a plan…'

Further Ideas

- If this work has piqued your student's interest in the original, direct him to Chapter II of *The Adventures of Tom Sawyer*.
- Choose a stand-in to play Ben. Working together, he and Tom can improvise lines for Ben during a rehearsal of the scene or write them together during quiet time. Ben arrives with a skip in his step. At first he scoffs at Tom for being forced to work. However, Tom's plan soon casts its spell. Encourage a strong performance so that Tom has plenty to play off. When you take Ben off the stage, can Tom maintain his focus?
- It is 'a lovely morning'; encourage Tom to imagine the warmth and beauty of his surroundings. How will his environment affect his movements?
- The fence is the focus of much of the scene's action. To have Tom facing front, you could run it along the front of the stage. Alternatively, it could run diagonally upstage to down.
- What exactly might the location look like? The book is set in a village in Missouri in the mid-1800s. Try an online image search for inspiration. Searches for 'Tom Sawyer' or 'Huckleberry Finn' return book illustrations and stills from film and TV adaptations. (See the cautionary note on page 9.)

One Thing at a Time

Lorna is taken by John Ridd, yet she knows the two of them are in mortal danger if they are found together by the approaching outlaws. Her emotions swing back and forth as she is torn between tending him and sending him away.

Younger actors tend to anticipate what is coming next, rushing to meet the next thought instead of letting it come to them. Practise playing one thing at a time.

Go through the scene slowly. Look for every moment when Lorna has a new feeling about her situation. At the top, before she speaks, she has found a boy on the ground. She might have seen him fall. She is rubbing his forehead. When he wakes up, she is relieved – she was worried that he was dead. There are two feelings: worry, then relief.

What thought is in Lorna's head when she is rubbing John's forehead? Ask your actor to give it a one- or two-word label. 'Dead Boy' would be a good choice. When he wakes up – but not until he wakes up – her new thought is 'Alive Boy!' Practise the opening of the scene. If you have a stand-in, tell him to leave it a while before waking up. In a solo class, you can signal the moment when John wakes. Lorna must be worried (by the thought 'Dead Boy') until the very moment when John wakes – and at that moment, she suddenly switches to the new thought ('Alive Boy') and the new feeling (relief).

Work through the scene, giving each new thought a label. For the first few lines, you might come up with this sort of sequence:

- *Dead Boy* • *Alive Boy* • *Who?* • *Wet Things* • *Only Fish*

Play through the sequence as a series of tableaux. Your actor takes the stage. Call out 'Dead Boy'; she strikes a pose, tending to John worriedly. Next call out 'Alive Boy'; she strikes a new pose in response to the new situation. Continue, exploring the sharp switches in Lorna's mind as things develop.

These sharp switches occur throughout the scene. One sequence runs:

- *We'll Die* • *Go Away* • *I Like You* • *Go Away* • *They're Coming.*

Break the scene up and work chunk by chunk, first in tableaux and then with words. Can your actor play as clearly and strongly on the text as off?

It is best if the ideas for those one- or two-word labels come from your actor. The more decisions she makes herself, the more ownership she'll have of her performance. But even if you take a lead in labelling each thought, she will choose how to express it on her face, in her body and with her voice.

Project Work

- CHARACTER WORKSHEET
- KNOWLEDGE NOTES
- STAGE DIAGRAM
- RESEARCH: Exmoor; book illustrations
- ART: Setting; annotated picture of John

GLOSSARY

outlaw	handkerchief	bear
knock out	kerchief	bind
tenderly	stockings	outright
dock leaf	bandage	

Source

The scene is adapted from R. D. Blackmore's 1869 novel *Lorna Doone*. Chapter VIII begins with John Ridd, already half-dead from cold and exhaustion, coming to after a fall; he wakes to find Lorna tending him. The perilous journey leading up to his fall takes up most of Chapter VII.

Lorna Doone is not typical primary-school reading matter. The events are told from John's point of view, so reading the original will not shed much extra light on Lorna's inner world. Nevertheless, the novel may be of interest to you and your student. The source certainly provides lots of information about the impact Lorna makes on John and about his own actions and responses. If you use a stand-in for John, you and he will have plenty to draw on.

If you do ask Lorna to read the source, give support. You could work on small sections of the chapter at a time and set quizzes to guide her reading:

- What immediately impresses John about Lorna (two things)?
- Later in life, whenever he sees an early primrose he is reminded of her. Why?
- How does John describe his own appearance?

A quiz on the source passage is available on the web page which accompanies this book.

Other ideas

- The novel dwells on another factor that makes an association between Lorna and John unthinkable: the gulf in social class between them. He is different from the people she usually mixes with. Why might Lorna ('a lady born') be fascinated by this rough boy?
- Ask your actor to highlight the text wherever Lorna demands information from John and wherever she gives him instructions. Though young and tender, Lorna has authority and is accustomed to being obeyed.
- Lorna's status and the period (1676) should be reflected in the performance.
- There is scope for plenty of variation in pace. Lorna has frenetic moments and contemplative moments. Ask her to walk around the room as she speaks the text, adjusting the speed of her walk to the speed of Lorna's thoughts. She races when Lorna's mind is racing and saunters when Lorna is reflective.
- Bear in mind that it is a February evening and there is snow on the ground.
- An image search for 'Lorna Doone book' returns interesting illustrations.

❋ TRANSITIONS ❋

*G*ive your young actors practice at going from one emotion to another. They pick two cards from a pile of emotion words – *shock* and *joy*, for example. They work out a pose and facial expression for each. Then they go from the first to the second slowly as you count to ten. Reduce the count to five, two, and a hand clap.

To add context, ask them to imagine a situation for a gradual transition. For example, a door handle turns . . . the door slowly creaks open... it's Father Christmas! For a sudden change: something lands on their hand – it's a £20 note!

Finally, add text. All students should be able to find examples in their scenes. Lorna slowly realises that the wet things in the bag (disgust) are only fish (amusement). She hears a noise (alertness) and immediately realises that her cousins are approaching (terror).

Every scene is a journey, not from beginning to end in a straight line, but on irregular stepping stones from one moment to the next. Ask students to map their journey through the scene.

The Race Is On!

At the centre of this scene is an exciting running race with mismatched opponents and an unlikely outcome. Here are a few enjoyable ways to engage your students with the situation:

- Draw a poster that will be pinned on trees throughout the woodland to advertise the race.
- Appoint a coach for each competitor. Ask them to discuss strategy for the race and feed back to the group.
- Stage a pre-race press conference (as a hot seating exercise). Other students are the journalists. Give them a little time to prepare questions to ask **Hare** and **Tortoise** (in a duo class, you ask the questions):
  - Are you in good shape?
  - Have you been on a special diet?
  - What training have you been doing?
  - Do you think you will win?
  - How will the conditions today affect the race?

Project Work

- CHARACTER WORKSHEET
- KNOWLEDGE NOTES
- STAGE DIAGRAM
- RESEARCH: Hares and tortoises; hares/rabbits; Aesop's fables
- OUTING: Woodland visit
- ART: Race poster; animal characteristics (Top Trump or Match Attax card); woodland setting; stepping stones

GLOSSARY

cocky	slyly	nap
confront	witness	sprint
determined	lair	constantly
clearing	all mouth	acknowledge
gasp	oblivious	applause
stubby	dart	plod
lithe	glance	fling
stamina	crouch	shake on it
resume	pathetic	munch
double up with laughter	disgust	

Setting

The last question encourages your actors to make choices about the setting. What terrain will Tortoise and Hare be racing over? What time of year is it? What is the weather like today? Investigate the setting:

- Students draw the location.
- Students visit a woodland and take photos or gather collage materials.
- Hare and Tortoise give you a guided tour of the woodland (see page 57).
  - The tourists might be animals considering moving into the area.
  - The tourists might be developers thinking of building a new road or sports centre. If the building goes ahead, residents receive a big cash bonus. So Tortoise and Hare need to 'sell' the area to their visitors.

Other Characters

If you have a group, choose stand-ins to play Mr. Rabbit, Mr. Fox and other woodland characters as required. (Distinguishing between a hare and a rabbit will be an interesting challenge that might need some research.) Any animal characters from other scenes should be included in the scene – it gives those actors an excellent opportunity to inhabit their character in a different scenario and without the pressure to speak lines.

Encourage stand-ins to commit to their performances: they can learn a great deal from this supporting work. They might improvise lines and can boo and cheer during and after the race. They should create strong characters and engage fully with the situation so that Hare and Tortoise have plenty to play off. Who do they want to win? What is their private opinion of the racers?

If the background performances are strong, when you remove the actors, they will leave their imprint on the scene.

Emotional Ups and Downs

Work with both actors on tracing the arc of the scene. Each should come up with five or six words to describe how they feel at key moments. Tortoise might choose exhausted, angry, confident, determined and happy. When they have chosen their words, they can:
- map the scene as stepping stones across a river; one word in each stone
- choose a colour for each word and highlight the script
- create a pose for each and play the scene as a series of tableaux.

Source

Ask your student to find out about the ancient Greek writer Aesop and his remarkable fables. One of the best online texts is the audio version on the BBC Learning School Radio website – which also includes teaching notes on the fables. There is a link on the web page which accompanies this book.

❊ PLAYING ANIMALS ❊

*T*he ability to play an animal is a fundamental skill for an actor to acquire. It is a unique challenge that requires a total transformation. Most drama school programmes require student actors to play animals at some point, and some include very prolonged investigations of animals in 'zoo' exercises. Many actors use animal techniques even when creating a human character by asking the question, 'If I were an animal, what animal would I be?'

There are animals throughout the Acting Anthology. If asked to play an animal, many young actors will drop onto all fours. Yet crawling is uncomfortable and restrictive. Insist that animals are upright. If your students are doubtful, you could mention any number of animal performances, from Paddington to Puss in Boots. Show clips of the stage version of The Lion King.

Here are a few ideas for developing an upright animal. Capturing the animal's physicality (the outer rhythm) will lead you into its character (the inner rhythm).
- If possible, first research the animal by observing real specimens or watching videos.
- Your actor comes up with a list of words to describe the physical qualities of, say, a tortoise (slow, sleepy, heavy, careful). Mine the scene for clues (Hare's arms are 'long and lithe').
- He walks around the room in neutral.
- As you call out the words one by one, he adds them into the walk until he is transformed.
- Now he imagines how someone who moves like that might talk. He comes to greet you.
- In a group, animals mingle and interact. Play a simple 'guess the animal' game.
- Consolidate the work with a drawing. You could expand the drawing into a Top Trump or Match Attax card for each character, focusing on personal qualities – both positive and negative. Each creature might be rated, for example, on speed, strength, intelligence, weapons, cuteness, and so on. In a big group, you might have enough cards for a start-of-lesson game.

Source

This scene has been adapted from a passage close to the beginning of Chapter 2 ('The New Friend') of Neil Gaiman's 2008 children's novel. If they have a taste for the gruesome and the spooky, your students should enjoy this book. Encourage them to read at least the relevant chapter, which will take them into **Bod**'s very weird world and enrich their understanding of him and **Scarlett**.

The source offers some ideas for staging the scene. It is a sunny spring day. Bod wears a grey winding sheet, while Scarlett is dressed in yellow, pink and orange. Although your actors must not wear full costume, having one drab and the other colourful would create a striking visual contrast. The source will provide plenty of inspiration for drawings of the characters and setting.

Project Work

- CHARACTER WORKSHEET
- KNOWLEDGE NOTES
- STAGE DIAGRAM
- OUTING: Graveyard (accompanied and in the daytime!)
- ART: Characters and setting
- WRITING: Postcard to your new friend

GLOSSARY

graveyard	gargoyle	fibber
raised	crease	enthusiastic
gorse	satisfied	tombstone
crumple	squint	

That's Easy!

Both characters have moments of self-confidence and moments of self-doubt. Scarlett knows she is an excellent face puller but struggles with spelling. Bod knows he is an excellent speller but has no idea how old he is. Practise these alternating feelings with a fun game:

- On cards, write ten or so difficult tasks. Examples might include:
  - ✦ Fly like a helicopter
  - ✦ Win *Britain's Got Talent*
  - ✦ Bake an ostrich pie
  - ✦ Speak Martian.
  - ✦ Wash a lion
- One actor says 'I don't know how to…' and reads a card at random. The other character replies 'That's easy!' and explains how.
- In a group, other students carry out the task, following the instructions.
- Switch a few times so Bod and Scarlett have a go at being both clueless and expert.

Improvisation: Enemies to Friends

At the beginning of the scene, Bod and Scarlett stick their tongues out at each other. By the end they are looking forward to seeing each other again. Practise this journey with an improvisation game.

Two players start as enemies and must become friends. Two minutes allows a short scene to develop; one minute adds a frenzied edge. Give your actors characters and a situation. Decide what outcome each wants:

- Two brainy Hogwarts pupils from enemy houses (Gryffindor and Slytherin) both want to be top of the class. They have been forced to work together on a spellmaking exercise.

- Two mild-mannered old ladies see a £20 note on the ground at exactly the same moment. Each believes it is hers and wants to put it in her purse.

- Fierce knights from opposing armies fight each other. Suddenly they find themselves both under attack by a dragon.

The progression from enemies to friends in this game can be sudden (as long as it is convincing), but here it would be better to match the journey of the scene by improvising a gradual coming together.

If it helps your students, count them through the scene. At 1 they are sworn enemies, and by 10 they are firm friends. At the midway point (5), they are lukewarm – neither hostile nor friendly.

FOLLOW-UP

- Now return to the text. Your actors stand opposite each other at a distance and speak the lines. Each time Scarlett says something negative about Bod, she steps backwards; each time she says something positive, she steps forwards. Bod does the same. What pattern of movement is there through the scene?
- Repeat the activity; this time, they step not only when they say something but also when they feel or think something negative or positive. As you work through, pause to analyse their choices.

Further Ideas

- Be clear about where Scarlett's mother is. During rehearsals, you (or another student) should shout so that the onstage actors have something to react to.
- A gargoyle game will make a fun warm-up. Get photos of gargoyles from a book or online image search. Print two copies of each to make two sets. A volunteer picks a picture at random from one set, looks at it secretly, and imitates the face. Classmates look at their set of pictures and guess which face he is doing.
- Use chairs for gravestones.

❋ IMPROVISATION ❋

*D*rama without improvisation is almost unthinkable. When it's done well, actors play with a gleeful spontaneity that work on the text rarely offers. A good improvisation can generate more ideas in two minutes than weeks of textual analysis.

Many young actors find improvisation in class difficult. Yet a playground is full of expert improvisers. Making it up as you go along is the way children naturally play. What are 'Mummies and Daddies' and 'Cops and Robbers' if not grand improvisations?

For an improvisation, tell each actor WHO she is, WHERE she is and WHAT she wants. If it is difficult for her to get what she wants (because of the obstacles in her way – see page 116), you'll have drama.

Give your actors a little time (but not too much) to absorb the bare bones. Then explain that nothing is expected of them. You have no idea what they're going to say or do, and nor do they. There is no aim for the exercise other than to play. They don't have to be funny or original, just to pretend. The scene can be rough, ragged, repetitive, rude or ridiculous. You just want to see what happens – which might be nothing.

The more practice your students have, the more happily they'll improvise. As times goes on, their improvisations will amaze and delight you.

SQUEAK AND MAIOW!

by L E McCullough ✳ *Acting Anthology page 33*

Animal Characters

The drama and comedy of this scene lie in the differences between **Cat** and **Rat**. Encourage your actors to find as many points of contrast between their characters as possible. Their differences could encompass:

- PHYSICALITY – MOVEMENT

  Ask your actors to research how their animal moves quickly, moves slowly, eats, rests, sleeps, swims, responds to danger and expresses happiness. They can do so either by observing a real specimen (such as a family pet) or by watching film footage. Ask each to write a list of words that describe the physical qualities of his animal. In class, use one word at a time to turn a neutral walk into an animal walk (see page 27).

- PHYSICALITY – RHYTHM

  Is each animal's movement fast or slow? Heavy or light? Smooth or jagged? Make sure your actors choose different combinations of these factors to give different overall rhythms.

- VOICE

  Once your actors are moving around the room in character, they can start making noises to see what sounds naturally emerge from the physicality they have developed. Ask them to yawn, sneeze, make a thinking noise, cry out in shock or pain (Cat has an 'Aiieee!' in the scene), eat something delicious (Rat has a 'yum-yum-yum-yum-yum') and so on. Move onto words – first ask simple questions that have one-word answers, and then be more conversational.

- PERSONALITY

  What qualities do writers usually give cats and rats? (Both animals can be found elsewhere in the Acting Anthology.) Are those qualities evident in this scene? How many opposites can your actors come up with to describe their characters? Is one brave and the other cowardly? One friendly and the other aggressive? Cheerful and serious? Relaxed and stressed?

Work on character can be recorded on a character worksheet (see page 85; samples can be downloaded from the web page which accompanies this book). Choices can also be fixed with an annotated drawing or spider diagram.

FOLLOW-UP

Cat and Rat have a very different view of events. Ask each to tell you or the class the story of the scene from his perspective. What has he learnt from the experience?

Project Work
- CHARACTER WORKSHEET
- KNOWLEDGE NOTES
- STAGE DIAGRAM
- RESEARCH: *Manioc root; cats and rats*
- OBSERVATION: *Feeling hungry*
- ART: *Character; spider diagram*

GLOSSARY

harmony	desperately	remark
satisfied	apparently	review
mainland	delirious	paradise
manioc root	startle	
sturdy	resemble	

Double Acts

Cat and Rat are fundamentally different characters who find themselves in the same critical situation. Can your students find points in the scene where the same situation provokes different responses? How does each character respond to imminent death? How does each cope with being hungry?

In the way they behave and interact, exasperated Cat and childish, carefree Rat are a classic double-act. They are versions of Laurel and Hardy, Morecambe and Wise, Father Dougal and Father Ted and many others.

It will be fun and also useful to show your students clips of double acts at work. The *Laurel and Hardy* shorts 'Them Thar Hills' and 'Tit for Tat' are full of entertaining interplay. *Father Ted* is not aimed at children, but clean clips available on YouTube at the time of writing include 'It's Not Morning' and 'On Holiday.' Plenty of Morecambe and Wise sketches are also available. Vet all clips for suitability before showing them (see page 9).

Sleeping and Waking

At the centre of this scene is a piece of clownish business: the two animals alternately sleep and wake, and Rat furtively gobbles a hole in the bottom of their manioc-root boat.

If you work on the choreography, you should get very amusing results. The sequence is as follows:

- Rat sleeps (pretend)
- Cat looks • Cat sleeps (snores)
- Rat wakes • Rat checks • Rat nibbles
- Cat wakes • Rat sleeps (pretend)
- Cat looks • Cat sleeps (snores)
- Rat wakes... and so on.

First, familiarise Rat and Cat with the sequence (if you have a group, put your students into Rat/Cat pairs). Play it through a few times: as you call each cue, they carry out the action. You could also find the right rhythm for the sequence by performing it to a metronome or regular tambourine beats.

Ask actors to work on their facial expressions – rat's mischievousness and cat's befuddlement are important for the humour of the scene. If they play the mischief and the befuddlement directly to the audience (as some of their lines are played), the scene will be very clownish.

Next, give Rat and Cat a bit of time to practise on their own before showing their sequence to you or the group.

Finally, add in the text. Work on the portion from Rat's line 'don't panic' to the moment when Cat wakes up, startled. Can your actors integrate the words into their comic routine?

Further Ideas

- Despite their harmonious living, is there any part of Cat that sees Rat as food? The line 'I'm sure hungry' might have an edge to it.
- What is the animals' mood at the top of the scene, just as they set out for their new life? What is the weather like? How long will the journey be? What do they hope to find on the mainland?

Source Text

This scene is adapted from the eighth chapter ('Trial by Fire') of *Emily of New Moon* (1923). Your actors may be familiar with Montgomery's *Ann of Green Gables* series. If they are keen readers, encourage them to read at least the relevant chapter of this novel. Doing so will take them into the world **Emily** and **Rhoda** inhabit.

Setting

The location is Blair Water, a small town on Prince Edward Island in eastern Canada. It is noon on a warm June day at the end of the nineteenth century.

An image search for 'Emily of New Moon' returns book illustrations and stills from a 1998 Canadian TV adaptation. These pictures will give your actors a sense of the period and location. For pictures of the specific setting for this scene, try searching for 'Prince Edward Island schoolhouse'. Make sure that any online research tasks, whether done in class or at home, are closely monitored (see page 9 for tips).

Emily is a newcomer in Blair Water, and this is her first day at school. It is clear to her that the girls have made up their minds to dislike her (she immediately senses the 'antagonistic' atmosphere). They resent her because her aunt is well-to-do. They assume Emily thinks herself better than them.

Game: Guide Me Home

Rhoda has the initiative throughout the scene. She is on home territory, and she drives the dialogue. Emily is friendless in an unfamiliar place.

A blindfold game will connect both actors with the power dynamic of the scene. Establish a trusting atmosphere before you begin. Explain the purpose of the game: to experience the feeling of not being in charge. Tell Emily that nobody will trick her and that you will be watching carefully to make sure she is safe. Before you start, describe the whole game.

- Blindfold Emily. So that she is comfortable, sit her with a friend.
- Set up an obstacle course of soft objects, with a chair at the end. Emily must reach the chair without touching any of the scattered objects.
- The actors stand, Rhoda in front of Emily. Emily takes Rhoda's elbow. Rhoda guides her through the course. No talking.
- Repeat (change the layout of the course). This time Rhoda and Emily, (side by side or facing each other) touch only the tips of one index finger. As Emily follows Rhoda through the course, they try to maintain contact.
- Repeat with no contact: Rhoda guides Emily with her voice only.

FOLLOW-UP
- Discuss the experience. How does it feel to hold all the power – or none?
- How can the power balance be reflected in the blocking of the scene?

The Truth About Rhoda

Rhoda apologises for her part in the mean trick and gushes with affection for Emily. But have your actors read between the lines and picked up the hollow ring to Rhoda's declarations of friendship? Her incessant questions revolve around one theme. Why is she trying to win Elizabeth's friendship?

If your students are reading the novel, they will soon find out the truth about Rhoda, which is revealed in the tenth chapter, called 'Growing Pains.'

Game: Truth and Lies

Rhoda swears she did not know there was a snake in the box. It is a lie (the whole ruse was Rhoda's idea). Yet she's a good liar: Emily believes her, as she seems to believe Rhoda's desire to be her friend.

It is difficult to act lying. Rhoda will need to identify her character's true wants, bury them deep inside and play the text as though she were speaking the truth. Those buried motives should lend subtle colour to her performance. A lying game will give her practice off the text. Can Emily winkle her out?
- Your actors list categories on a piece of paper, leaving space underneath each. This must not be information the girls know about each other:
  - Foods I don't like
  - Countries I've visited
  - Names of my cuddly toys
  - Presents I got for my last birthday
- They write three answers for each. Two must be true, one a plausible lie.
- They play as themselves, not in character. Emily asks Rhoda 'What foods don't you like?' Rhoda gives her three answers. Can Emily spot the lie?
- After you've reversed the roles, follow up by discussing how it feels to tell a lie – and how (if at all) you can spot when someone else is lying.
- Develop this exercise on the text. Find Rhoda's first lie: 'Emily, I'm awfully sorry.' Ask her to enjoy (privately) watching Emily fling the snake away in horror. Remind her how much she dislikes Emily. Now she approaches Emily and apologises as sincerely as she can.

DEVELOPMENT: THE VOICE OF TRUTH

Use another actor, if you have a group, to play Rhoda's inner voice:
- Rhoda and Emily take the stage; Rhoda's inner voice stands to the side, at a short distance from Rhoda. Underneath the onstage dialogue, the inner voice expresses Rhoda's true thoughts and intentions.
- For example, as Rhoda says that she didn't know there was a snake in the box, her inner voice sniggers and gleefully says it was all her idea.
- When Rhoda tells Emily she likes her, the inner voice hisses that she hates Emily.
- Work through the scene. Can Rhoda 'hear' the inner voice even when you take the other actor away?

Further Idea

The girls should play this period scene in practice skirts (see page 121).

APPLE SCRAMBLE
by Clare Price ❋ Acting Anthology page 39

Silent Scene

This scene involves lots of movement and business for both **Judy** and **Mary**. You could work on the physical action first and bring in the dialogue later.

First, help your actors to grasp the scene's structure. Choose ten or twelve key pieces of action, such as:

- Judy climbs over the wall.
- Mary lets go of the branch.
- Mary sees a bull.

Write the actions on separate pieces of paper and ask your actors to put them in the correct order.

When you have your sequence, add in any other major actions you think are necessary to make a skeleton for the scene. Set the scripts aside. The actors take the stage. As you call out each action, they perform it. Encourage them to stay in character throughout so there is a continuous line through the sequence.

Repeat, refining and adding more detail: Judy's opening grimace, the business with the bags, the failed attempts to grab the branch, and so on. As your actors become familiar with the sequence, the story should fill out. The characters' differing actions and reactions will become clear, and their feelings towards each other and the situation will emerge.

When you have a more or less complete silent scene, ask them to perform it straight through. Is the story clear to you (or watching classmates)? Is it obvious that Judy is hungry? That Mary is a better jumper? That it is a bull?

Project Work

- CHARACTER WORKSHEET
- KNOWLEDGE NOTES
- STAGE DIAGRAM
- OBSERVATION: Eating an apple
- OUTING: Countryside walk / apple tree
- ART: Make a silent movie; draw the setting; Ted Gilly
- WRITING: Lamb advert

GLOSSARY

scramble	spoil sport	nonchalantly
grimace	admire	nip
sarcastically	retrieve	scowl
sponsor	excessive	
private property	foothold	

DEVELOPMENT: SILENT MOVIE

It would be fun to choose suitable accompanying music and to play the scene as a silent movie. For inspiration, watch some silent film sequences with your actors – try a YouTube search for Buster Keaton, Charlie Chaplin or Harold Lloyd (and bear in mind the note on internet safety on page 9).

For added fun, you could record your silent movie. There are smartphone or tablet video apps that will do most of the hard work for you.

The Art of Persuasion

In the first part of the scene, Judy tries to convince Mary to help her steal some apples. Every time Judy pleads, Mary's (usually wordless) response is 'no'. Every time Mary refuses, Judy tries a different approach until she eventually succeeds. Work with your actors on drawing out Judy's various strategies so that there is plenty of variety in her speeches.

First, find all of the reasons Judy gives for stealing the apples:

- I'm starving.
- I'm on a diet for charity.
- The apples are right there.
- The apples are nice and juicy.
- It will be easy.
- We've done it before.
- They grow wild.
- I'm starving!
- You're a spoil sport.

Some of Judy's arguments are forceful, and some are seductive. Number the arguments from 1–9. 1 is fully forceful: Judy implies that Mary is being really silly. 9 is fully seductive: Judy implies that she is really suffering.

Explore this tussle actively. The girls take the stage. Judy voices the nine arguments above, in turn. Each time, Judy answers 'no', until she finally answers 'Okay'. Try the following variations:

- Every time Mary says 'no', she turns to face a different direction. Judy must move around and make eye contact before trying again.
- The girs face each other, palms touching. As Judy pleads, she pushes Mary backwards. The more forceful she is being, the stronger she pushes. Mary answers 'no' and pushes Judy back to her starting point.
- Stage an arm wrestle or a tug-of-war along the same lines. Or give the girls a balloon each. Judy accompanies each plea with a firm bop on Mary's head. Mary responds with 'no' and a bop back.
- Scripts will impede these games. Quietly feed Judy her words.

Follow up with a discussion. Were there times when Mary almost said yes? Why does she finally say yes? Is she worried about being a spoil sport?

Character Work

Your actors are free to make a lot of choices about their characters. Always start with the facts, however scant: the scene tells you that Judy is sensitive (she felt sorry for the lamb), has willpower (she gave up meat), takes risks and recovers quickly from shocks (such as a charging bull). Mary is cautious, more athletic than Judy and enjoys a sunny day. From this basis, your actors should complete a character worksheet and draw their character. You could then put them in the hot seat (see page 10) and ask them about their home and school life, favourite memories, hopes for the future and so on.

Further Ideas

- Break the scene into chapters and give each a title. Where does the scene shift in a new direction, signalling the start of a new chapter? For each chapter, can the actors decide what is their character's strongest feeling about their situation? For more on breaking scenes up, see page 70.
- What happened immediately before this scene? What does Judy mean by 'Come on, Mary'? Ask your actors to improvise a prequel, starting from when Judy and Mary leave the school gate.
- Miming eating an apple is difficult, so practise. Video your actors eating a real apple. How do they hold it, bite it, chew and swallow? Video them miming. Do they convince? See page 104 for further tips on miming.
- Judy has been moved by an advert (presumably on TV) featuring a lamb. What was the advert? Script (or improvise) it. One actor plays the lamb.
- Draw Ted Gilly in his field.

Source

Unless they are very reluctant readers, your actors will be happy for an opportunity to read (or reread) Roald Dahl's children's book, first published in 1980. This episode, one in a series of tit-for-tat tricks the couple play on each other, can be found in the eighth and ninth chapters ('The Funny Walking-stick' and 'Mrs Twit Has the Shrinks').

Project Work

- CHARACTER WORKSHEET
- KNOWLEDGE NOTES
- STAGE DIAGRAM
- ART: *Ugly gallery; other character*
- WRITING: *Ugly thoughts and disgusting sentences*

GLOSSARY

constantly	foot	pistol
practical joke	in comparison	bundle
mutual	trembly	grizzly
convince	dangle	

Ugly Thoughts

Mrs Twit had a nice face when she was young but has grown into a fearsomely ugly woman. If your actors read the book's fourth chapter, they'll discover why: 'if a person has ugly thoughts, it begins to show on the face.' You could use this idea as a basis for physically characterising the pair. What face might your actors pull if they were thinking of doing something mean or horrible? What would happen to their body?

First, list some ugly thoughts each Twit has about the other:

- I'm going to make **Mr Twit** eat worms.
- I'm going to put a frog in Mrs Twit's bed.
- I'm going to hit Mr Twit with my stick.
- I'm going to send Mrs Twit to the moon.

Your actors add five more mean tricks each Twit might play. They take the stage and mime a simple task, such as tidying or drawing. They begin in neutral. You read the first ugly thought, and the actor expresses its horribleness through the whole body. The change is permanent. Read the next thought and the next. Each snarl, grimace or contortion is added to the last.

At the end of the exercise, they keep the physicality they have developed and walk around the space. Give them actions from the scene – for Mr Twit, picking up a stick and examining it; for Mrs Twit, feeling trembly and sitting down. Are characters emerging? How might they speak? Ask them a few simple questions with one-word answers. Then feed in lines from the script.

FOLLOW-UP

- A good drawing task would be an ugly gallery: actors draw a series of pictures of their character at various stages of life, from the good-looking young children they once were to the ugly adults they now are.
- Each actor can also draw the other's character. Add annotations. All of the hatred they have for each other can be channeled into these pictures.

Character: You're Disgusting!

Each Twit thinks the other is disgusting. Any of these games gives students an opportunity to be disgusting as well as to engage with the Twits' world:

DISGUSTING SOUP

Everyone sits in a circle. Place an imaginary pot in the centre and say that your favourite meal is disgusting soup. When you eat it, you turn into a Twit and become disgusting. After a minute it wears off and you need a nap.

You got started before the class, and the stinging-nettle stock is ready. Try some; it's a bit prickly but tastes much too nice. In turn, each student puts in a disgusting ingredient. As they stir the soup with a huge spoon, everyone repeats the ingredient and says 'yum, yum, yum.' After everyone has had a go, try a sip, say its perfect, and ladle out bowlfuls. With each spoonful your students become more and more disgusting until they are a full-blown Twit. They move disgustingly around the space. At your signal they start to feel weary, and by the count of ten they collapse, exhausted.

You're sure to get poo, wee and vomit. If you outlaw them (or allow them only once each), you'll clear the way for more imaginative ideas.

FOUL CONSEQUENCES

Prepare several incomplete sentences about each Twit along these lines:

- In the morning, Mr Twit smells like…
- Mrs Twit's face reminds me of…
- Mr Twit picked his nose and out came…
- I saw Mrs Twit eating…

Hand out pieces of paper. Ask your students to recall and write down the ingredients that went into Disgusting Soup. Put the pieces into a hat.

Stick your incomplete sentences on the wall. Students in turn take a sentence, read it and complete it with a random word drawn from the hat.

Follow up by asking Mr Twit to write down all the sentences about Mrs Twit and vice versa. These can sit alongside their drawings of each other.

SHRINKING DISEASE

This game has fear as well as disgust. Playing it will engage Mrs Twit with the rising panic she feels at the deterioration in her health. It's a good warm-up.

Stand the class in a circle and ask them sombrely whether they've read the news: shrinking disease has broken out in the area. It's highly contagious, and if anyone has brought it into the room, you're all for it. The disease progresses rapidly through ten increasingly severe symptoms. The tenth and fatal symptom is a sudden shrinking to nothing, accompanied by despairing screams. Invent the first nine (or take ideas from the group). Symptoms should start mildly (itchy elbows, say) and get wilder (gnashing teeth, uncontrollable flapping, hysterical monkeys) before climaxing with death.

Ask the class to spread out. Dismay your students by experiencing the first symptom yourself. The disease is in the room and they will all suffer. Call out the symptoms one by one until everyone screams and dies together.

Setting

Roald Dahl says little about the Twits' house except that it is windowless, like a prison. Your students are free to imagine all the disgusting details of the setting. Only Mrs Twit's old chair is specified. Students will be asked to describe the location in the Knowledge section of their LAMDA exam, so they can practise by taking you on a guided tour (see page 57).

Weddings

Each actor should have a very clear mental image of herself as a bridesmaid at a wedding. **Rosie**'s mind is filled with the wedding she has just attended (and is now reliving), and **Jessica**'s with the wedding she longs to attend. If either girl has been to a wedding (especially as a bridesmaid), quiz her about it and ask to see photos. Focus on appearances (as Rosie does), by asking what everything looked like and what everyone wore.

There are other ways to help your actors conjure up the mental images they will draw on in performance:

- Get hold of some bridal magazines. Ask each girl to find her favourite dress, vehicle, location, smile and so on. In class or at home, they can make a collage of favourite pictures.
- Watch some movie wedding scenes. Plenty are available to view on YouTube – try *Father of the Bride, Four Weddings and a Funeral* or *Tangled*. You could also watch footage of the 2011 wedding of Prince William to Kate Middleton. Vet all clips for suitability first (see page 9).
- Show them your own wedding photos if you have them.

Project Work

- CHARACTER WORKSHEET
- KNOWLEDGE NOTES
- STAGE DIAGRAM
- RESEARCH: *Movie wedding scenes*
- OUTING: *Wedding!*
- ART: *Wedding collage; Rosie's three weddings; wedding invitation; setting*

GLOSSARY

bridesmaid	curtsy	green with envy
revel	almond	sweep
envious	satin	cheque
yearn	lacy	bribery
sedately	petticoats	contemptible
longingly	twirl	lecture
halo	cut in	
long	daintily	

Angel and Demon

The girls' emotions are high, and the dialogue is filled with subtext that needs to be investigated. As an active way of delving into the text, play the scene in different ways so that you and your actors can discover what feels right.

First, they play the scene as though Rosie is an angel, gentle and truthful, and Jessica is a demon, spiteful and treacherous. They must stick to these roles, even when the script seems to be pushing in a different direction:

- Rosie wants to share a joyous experience with her best friend. If you're happy, you shouldn't keep it to yourself. Poor Jessica hasn't been a bridesmaid yet, but hopefully she will be one day.
- Jessica can't bear it when Rosie is happy and wants to puncture that balloon. She tells a nasty lie that will destroy Rosie's pretty little memories.

Now your actors swap; Rosie is the demon, Jessica the angel:

- Rosie knows how desperately Jessica wants to be a bridesmaid. She wants to make Jessica feel as jealous as it is possible to be.
- Jessica is happy because her best friend is happy. But as Rosie's friend, Jessica wants to teach her that it's wrong to be wrapped up in your appearance and wrong to rely on money to get you what you want.

❋ LEARNING LINES (1) ❋

Students at every LAMDA exam grade are assessed on their ability to 'perform from memory with fluency and focus'. Failing to learn lines properly is the most common reason students fail Acting exams. Fluffing lines and taking prompts brings down marks. If an actor is secure in her lines – she knows them and knows that she knows them – she will perform with freedom.

Learning lines takes hard work and practice. Visual, auditory and kinaesthetic learning techniques will suit different actors. No single method works best. Here are a few to try out:

- Go chunk by chunk. Read the first sentence, speak it aloud, cover it, speak it again, check. When you've got it, move on to the next sentence. Then take the two sentences together. Learn the third on its own, then practise all three together. When the chunk is learnt, move on.
- Look for poetic patterns – alliteration, rhyme, rhythm – that will glue phrases in the mind: **b**asket of **b**eautiful **b**eautiful roses; **p**retty **p**retty almond **p**ink; haven't **sh**own you my **sh**oes.
- In a big speech, understand the progressions from one thought to the next: bridesmaid three times > professional > first silk > second satin > Saturday this.
- Record a scene and listen to it many times. Record another version with gaps for your lines. Speak your lines in the gaps, checking with a script. (Or use a specialised smartphone or tablet app – for a list of suggestions, see the web page which accompanies this book.)
- Reading your script, copy out your lines. The act of writing may help you to learn them. Bit by bit, read, cover and write again. When you've finished, check for mistakes, then try again.
- Practise your lines while doing something that engages the brain's motor function, such as bouncing a ball against a wall, skipping or doodling.

For more on learning lines, see page 71. Note, too, the vital importance of focus: if an actor maintains the character and situation, small slips on the lines might go unnoticed.

Take feedback from your actors (and audience). They will probably conclude that each scene felt right at certain moments and wrong at others. Neither character is entirely angelic or demonic. They have subtly mixed motives.

Does Jessica think Rosie is pretty? Does Rosie know how badly Jessica would love to be a bridesmaid? Is Rosie's sympathy overegged or sincere? Does Rosie cut Jessica off on purpose because she knows what Jessica is going to say? Did Jessica's Mum really make that accusation about the cheque? Is it true? These are the sorts of questions this exercise throws up.

Setting

No location is specified, but Rosie has dressed up in her bridesmaid's outfit, so the girls are likely to be in her bedroom. Your actors should spend some time 'designing' the room. They can draw a picture, make a model (out of cardboard, Lego, doll's house furniture) or use the stage itself. There are apps and online tools which allow you to design a room in 2D and then 'view' it in 3D. For a list of suggestions, see the web page which accompanies this book.

When the room is ready, Rosie and Jessica can give you (and classmates) a guided tour. How long has this been Rosie's bedroom? Has it been recently redecorated? Is it messy or tidy? Does Jessica spend a lot of time here? How does she feel when she is here? Is it very different from her own bedroom?

Wherever you set the scene, make sure your actors can explain and justify their choice in the Knowledge section of their exam.

EXTINCT
by Jacqueline Emery ✳ *Acting Anthology page 47*

Incompatibility

At the start of the scene, **Jamie** hates **Jack**, and Jack does not think highly of Jamie. If your actors can find reasons for their mutual dislike, their opening exchanges will have tension, and the journey to friendship will be dramatically interesting.

Have the boys had a specific falling out? The text doesn't provide details, but the actors could invent one. The text does suggest that the boys have different temperaments. Have your actors spotted that Jack is more bookish, while Jamie is more active? Develop these differences and generate more ideas with a simple questionnaire. Jamie and Jack work together, coming up with different answers to questions such as these:

- What's your favourite thing to do on a Saturday afternoon?
- What pictures do you have on your bedroom wall?
- What film have you watched the most times?

Once they have answered, give them a second sheet with inverted questions:

- What's your least favourite thing to do on a Saturday afternoon?
- What pictures would you never put on your bedroom wall?
- What the worst film you've ever seen?

This time, they copy the answers from each other's first sheet. In this way, the characters have opposite tastes – a good reason for them not to get along.

Hot-seat your actors (see pages 10 and 113). Ask Jack one of the questions. When he answers, Jamie disapproves. Explore their differences and set them at odds by encouraging them to argue over who is right.

How might appearance, voice and physicality reflect their differences?

Harmony and Disharmony

Give both actors a clean copy of the script and a highlighter. Each highlights lines in which he expresses negative feelings about the other. Jamie's first speech would be highlighted, as would his hitting Jack with the kitchen roll. Jack's 'small brain' and 'silly' jibes would be highlighted.

Next give them a different colour to highlight lines in which they are positive about each other, agree or are cooperating.

Finally, ask them to look at lines they have left un-highlighted and make a decision either way. Is Jamie's line 'You sound like an encyclopedia' insulting or admiring? Does a pattern emerge? Is there a definite point at which the boys set aside their differences, or does the animosity linger? There is no single right answer, but it is important that your actors make choices.

Project Work

- CHARACTER WORKSHEET
- KNOWLEDGE NOTES
- STAGE DIAGRAM
- RESEARCH: Dinosaurs
- OBSERVATION: Working under pressure
- ART: Dinosaur; setting
- WRITING: Character questionnaire

GLOSSARY

sulkily	encyclopaedia	admire
full of himself	vegetarian	handiwork
feet	plasticine	lop-sided
tons	triumphantly	insistently

DEVELOPMENT FOR A GROUP

Can the rest of the group tell when Jamie and Jack are at odds and when they are in tune? Ask classmates to make two simple signs. One represents 'enemies' and one represents 'friends'. Red and green 'lollipops' (card circles taped to pencils) would work well. As they watch Jamie and Jack play the scene, spectators hold up either sign according to the mood they pick up from the action. Does everyone agree? Can (or should) changes be made?

Race Against the Clock

The boys do not have long to make their dinosaur. Once they get going, their movement should be busy and pressured. Practise with a fun game:

- Split the class into two teams, Jamie on one team, Jack on the other.
- Jumble up a set of word cards (all the words should be objects).
- Pick a word at random and show it to Jamie and Jack.
- The boys race to…
  - draw the word
  - make a model (plasticine or Lego)
  - shape teammates into a 3D object.
- The first team to shout out the word wins a point.
- In a duo class, the boys have ten seconds to draw or make the word, and you judge which is best.

Follow up by discussing how working within a strict time limit affects movement and mood.

Setting

Where are the boys making their dinosaur? In a corner of the class? In the hall? Discuss the possibilities and make a clear choice. What furniture is in the room? How is it decorated? What temperature is it? Are there other people? A stage diagram will record all your actors' decisions.

❋ PROPS ❋

On one hand, the dinosaur making is central to this scene, and the craft materials (sticky tape, toilet roll tubes, etc) are specified in the dialogue and the stage directions.

On the other hand, having your actors make a dinosaur under exam conditions adds great pressure and risk. What is important about their exam performance is not the resulting dinsoaur; it is how well they convey character and situation. They are not truly Jack and Jamie in a classroom, they are acting. No amount of plasticine and pipe cleaners changes that fact.

If you give Jamie and Jack all their fact cards and craft materials (or the Mad Hatter a 24-piece porcelain tea set), your actors have a real job to set the stage beforehand and clear it afterwards, and their focus will be drawn away from the acting. You also risk overrunning the allotted time, ruining the timetable for the session and making life difficult for your examiner.

For prop-heavy scenes, you could mime all the business and focus everything on the acting. You could use one or two key props and mime the rest. You could use all the props in rehearsal, as you're creating and exploring the situation, and then take them out as the exam approaches.

Making the dinsoaur during a rehearsal would be instructive. A pre-made dinosaur could later be used in the exam, when Jack and Jamie can mime making it. Using a pen to draw on the final touches (the eyes and mouth) in the exam itself might be a nice touch (and not stressful).

See also the box about costume on page 121.

Booting Up

A stiff march and a metallic voice is fine, but the actor playing **Robot** can stretch himself further. If he starts from scratch and makes positive acting choices (instead of slipping into a ready-made stereotype), he will have ownership of the character he creates. His performance will be more interesting for him and his audience.

This physical exercise gets students thinking in general terms about robots. It's a good warm-up for any class:

- Your students are robots. You will switch them on, and they will perform their boot routine, testing their functions one by one.
- Explain that this is an exercise in body control; you want to see how well they can move just one part of the body at a time.
- They find a space and power down: feet together, arms hanging by the sides, chin on chest. Shoulders and toes relaxed. The robots are asleep.
- At your signal, they switch on. First they test their neck. Slowly lift the head. Look all the way to the left, then front, then right, then front again.
- Next test an arm. Raise a shoulder and lower it. Make a fist then uncurl the fingers. Bend the elbow to create a right angle in the arm, then practise a slow handshake. Drop the hand and repeat with the other arm.
- Work around the body and finish with a walk.
- Ambient music will create an atmosphere and encourage slow movement (see page 107 for thoughts on using music in a drama class).

Project Work

- CHARACTER WORKSHEET
- KNOWLEDGE NOTES
- STAGE DIAGRAM
- ART: *Robot drawing; robot advert; Customer; setting*
- WRITING: *Robot advert (film); full phone conversation*

GLOSSARY

customer	tosh
malfunction	mind the gap
man overboard	phoney
red alert	keep your hair on
batten down the hatches	good riddance

I, Robot

Next think in more detail. Robot's precise function will affect his appearance. What sort of a guard robot is he? How does he keep the family safe? From what dangers? Your students can work actively to figure out the robot's shape. **Customer** designs and moulds his partner into the robot he ordered.

- They set the robot in motion so that it can practise carrying out its tasks.
- As the robot moves around, it can find its voice by commentating on or describing its own actions.

Finally, your actors present the robot to you. They follow up (in class or at home) by drawing and naming their design.

IN A GROUP

Creating a robot will be fun for everyone in a class, so if circumstances and time allow, make it a group task. Divide the class into robot/designer pairs. When designs are complete…

- Designers present their robots to an audience of scientists
- Everyone draws the robots to make a robot gallery
- Draw a poster advert for the robot
- Script a filmed advert for the robot. Decide how the advert will be used (in-app, YouTube, TV) to determine length. Perform and film it.

Customer

Who is Customer? His or her back story is almost completely up for grabs. Start with the text. What facts does it provide?:

- Customer feels responsible for keeping the family safe
- He therefore ordered a guard robot
- The robot does not work. Customer phoned straight away to complain

After the facts come the deductions about his personality:

- He is not meek – he is trying to fix the problem rather than accepting it.
- He is angry when the trick is revealed and makes a wry joke

As long as there is nothing to contradict these facts and deductions, your actor can decide all of Customer's biographical details and back story. Encourage him to make bold choices in order to create a distinctive character that he can grasp hold of and believe in. All of his ideas should be channeled onto a character worksheet and into pictures of the character and the scene.

Ronnie

The twist in the tale comes when the robot reveals that he is in fact a man called Ronnie who has been pretending to be a robot.

Practise transforming from robot to human over a count of ten. Maximise contrast by making the human pose loose and floppy. The transformation might happen joint by joint. Or the whole body might gradually derobotise. Repeat over a count of five, then two, then in an instant.

The Voice on the Other End of the Phone

Customer should script the other half of the phone conversation so that he can listen and react to what Mick is saying to him. What might Mick have said when Customer replies 'Of course I want to keep my family safe!'?

Play the script through with him to check the flow.

Play the scene with all three characters. Ronnie/Robot speaks over Mick's lines and does his best to disrupt the conversation.

Further Ideas

- Where does this scene take place?
- Might Robot be moving around (and causing disruption)?
- How do your students explain the whole Robots-R-Us ruse? Ask them to spend some time together working out the corporate strategy.
- The malfunctioning Robot is apparently scrolling through its alert messages. What situation was each message designed for? The answers should give your actor some ideas for ways of playing the lines, as well as for accompanying movements.
- Practise the timing of the trip at the end of the scene.

Mine the Text

Probably the first decision your actors will want to make is who this mystery VIP is. Ask them to mine the text for every piece of information it offers about this event:

- It is a 'once in a lifetime' visit from this person to this place.
- It is something to tell your grandchildren about.
- The visit is being televised.
- It is the subject of a school project.
- It is 'part of History.'
- The famous visitor is in a Rolls Royce as part of a motorcade.
- This is someone you would wave a flag at.
- Plastic flags are on sale in shops.
- There are adults in the crowd. Someone might want to shoot this visitor.

Ultimately, whether your actors decide the visitor is the Queen of Denmark or Justin Bieber is not of huge consequence for the scene. The exercise is useful because it gives practice at mining the text – an important skill for an actor – and gets them talking about where the scene is set and elements of the background, such as their school and home life.

Project Work

- CHARACTER WORKSHEET
- KNOWLEDGE NOTES
- STAGE DIAGRAM
- OUTING: Real-life VIP visit!
- ART: School project elements: flags; pictures of the VIP
- WRITING: School project elements: biography of the VIP; interview; opinions, weather forecast

GLOSSARY

VIP	half-heartedly	dejected
cavalcade	macs	kerbside
dejected	shrug	Rolls Royce
spectators	cross-eyed	furiously
once in a lifetime	appropriate	swift

✳ DRAWING IN DRAMA CLASSES ✳

Drawing is a calm, reflective way for young actors to imagine the world of a scene. Groups will cherish drawing time, chattering contentedly and enjoying one another's efforts.

Free children from the pressure to draw 'well'. Let them scribble or be abstract. Ask them to represent their character's feelings with coloured splodges. Or give them magazines, scissors and glue and ask them to make a collage of their scene. Round off drawing with a chat – ask your students to show their work and share their thinking. Avoid offering judgement. The process is more important than the result. You are interested in their ideas, not their draughtsmanship.

Drawing pictures builds up a vivid back story. This will enrich a performance, and spontaneity exercises (hot-seating, thought tracking, improvisation, etc) will be easier and more enjoyable.

If you have set creative tasks such as the project suggested for this scene, your actors will have a record of the term's work. They will be able to reflect back on the work not merely as weekly coaching sessions for an Acting exam but as a much deeper creative process. They have explored a story, invented a character and inhabited an imaginary world.

Setting creative homework is a good way of ensuring your students spend time between classes thinking about their scenes. Make sure all supporting work is kept in a folder. A project folder will be a source of pride and will boost your students' ownership of their characters.

School Project

In quiet time, your actors can create the school project. Pages could include:

- an illustrated biography of the celebrity (this could be a collage using photos sourced online or from magazines)
- a route map of the journey the motorcade will take
- a poster advertising the visit
- an interview with the VIP discussing the visit
- opinions from those who think the visit is a bad idea
- a weather forecast for the day.

The flags would be a manageable prop for the exam performance and are important enough to include. It would be fun to make them.

Your actors can use a real celebrity or invent one.

For the location of the scene, your actors can use their real school and home town, borrow from a favourite book… or just invent.

Drama is Conflict

Examine the opposing attitudes Nicky and Toni express towards this visit.

- On a clean copy of the scene, use different colours to highlight positive and negative comments about the visit. Does a pattern emerge?
- Is it a question of temperament? Is Nicky generally the gloomier one?
- Do some thought tracking: run the scene; at your signal the actors freeze. Unfreeze one and ask her what is happening and how she is feeling.
- Lay out felt-tip pens on a table. Ask Toni to choose 'positive' colours and Nicky to choose 'negative' colours. Then each draws a picture of the visit. It can be a literal representation or an abstract mood picture.

Wants

What does each character want from this situation? If they can answer this question, your actors will find a link between what they say and what they feel. Their different feelings throughout the scene will be joined up to give them a through-line (a continuous emotional journey).

- Nicky might want to make Toni feel sorry for her.
- Nicky might want to persuade Toni that they should give up and go home.
- Toni might want to cheer Nicky up.
- Toni might want Nicky to share her enthusiasm about the visit.

Relationship

Mine the text for facts about the characters' relationship. Both refer to 'my Mum', so they are not sisters. Nicky made a flag, but Toni didn't, so they are probably in different classes or at different schools. They seem quite equal and go home together at the end. Beyond that, your actors can invent everything – their history; shared experiences; similarities and differences; private opinions of each other, and so on. You could let them figure it out quietly on their own, hot-seat them (see pages 10 and 113) or jump into an improvisation.

Further Idea

In a group class, have a cheering, jostling crowd to create the situation.

INTERPRETATION – 20 marks for each scene (40 total)
L01 Perform two scenes from memory, demonstrating an understanding of the material.

Does your student...	**Pass**	**Merit**	**Distinction**
Understand the MEANING of the words he is speaking?	Some	Most	All
Communicate the meaning of the words?	Some	Most	All
Understand the CHARACTER and the SITUATION?	Some of the time	Most of the time	All of the time
Communicate the character and the situation?	Some of the time	Most of the time	All of the time
Know the LINES?	Quite well	Well	Perfectly
Stay IMMERSED in the imaginary world?	Some of the time	Most of the time	Throughout

TECHNIQUE – 20 marks for each scene (40 total)
L02 Use vocal skills in response to the text.
L03 Use the performance space in response to the text.

Does your student...	**Pass**	**Merit**	**Distinction**
PROJECT (speak clearly and with appropriate volume)?	Some of the time	Most of the time	All of the time
PAUSE for thought or to let unseen characters speak?	Some of the time	Most of the time	All of the time
Vary PACE to express different emotions?	Some of the time	Most of the time	All of the time
Use appropriate MOVEMENT in the performance?	Some of the time	Most of the time	All of the time

KNOWLEDGE – 20 marks overall (conversation with the examiner)
L04 Know and understand the characters and situations in the chosen scenes.

Can your student discuss...	**Pass**	**Merit**	**Distinction**
The FEELINGS of both characters during the scenes?	Briefly	Securely	In detail
The LOCATION of both scenes?	Briefly	Securely	In detail
What both characters ARE DOING during the scenes?	Briefly	Securely	In detail

Distinction: 80–100 • Merit 65–79 • Pass: 50–64

A learner fails if

- He scores 49 marks or less overall OR
- He scores 0 in one or more of the assessment criteria (L01, L02 etc)

FORMAT: SOLO EXAMS (15 MINUTES ALLOWED) AND DUOLOGUE EXAMS (20 MINUTES)

- 1 set scene from the *LAMDA Acting Anthology, Volume 3*
- 1 own-choice scene (between 2 and 3 minutes)
- Conversation

FORMAT: COMBINED EXAMS (25 MINUTES ALLOWED)

- 1 set duologue from the *LAMDA Acting Anthology, Volume 3*
- 2 own-choice solo scenes (between 2 and 3 minutes each)
- Conversation… OR
- 2 set solo scenes from the *LAMDA Acting Anthology, Volume 3*
- 1 own-choice duologue (between 2 and 3 minutes)
- Conversation

Scenes may be performed in any order.

Learners must announce the title, author and character of each scene before performing it. Decide on the phrasing and practise plenty of times:

- *For my set scene, I will be performing… by… I am playing the part of…*
- *My own-choice scene is… by… and I will be playing…*

Consider including a brief (one- or two-sentence) explanation of the context if your actors can manage it. It shows they have thought about their scene and adds polish to their performance. If an own-choice scene is not familiar to the examiner, the context will be useful.

Get students to test each other.
Recruit parents and siblings to help at home.
Explore different **line-learning** techniques.
Work on picking up **cues**.

Go through the glossary.

Walk around the room, varying speed according to the character's emotional energy (see page 25). Look for high-tempo feelings (excitement, panic) and low-tempo feelings (sadness, exhaustion).

Insist on no peeking (see page 87).

Use **circle time** for conversation practice.

Sit at the back of the room during run-throughs.
Close your eyes during runs: can you hear the words?
Do regular **voice** exercises and **tongue-twisters**.

Look at **transitions** from one feeling or idea to the next. Make sure each thought occupies its own space (see page 24).

Work on physical characterisation. You read the words while the actor mimes the scene. Do some **tableau** exercises.

During runs, freeze and do **thought tracking.**
Do abstract drawings or colour the script using **colours for feelings.**
Do plenty of **hot seating.**

CHECKLIST: GRADE 2

Do you…
- ☐ know your lines?
- ☐ understand all of the words?
- ☐ project (a strong clear voice)?
- ☐ use pauses?
- ☐ vary the pace?
- ☐ move during the scene?
- ☐ stay in character?

Can you describe…
- ☐ your character's feelings?
- ☐ the location of the scene?
- ☐ your character's actions?

Complete a stage diagram.
Do a guided tour (see page 57).
Make a picture of the setting.

Look at the character's **wants.**
Divide the scene into **chapters.**
Read the words while your student performs the **actions.**

*Words in **bold** text can be found in the index.*

JANE EYRE

adapted by LAMDA from Charlotte Brontë ❋ *Acting Anthology page 57*

Situation: Source Text

This short but highly charged scene is adapted from Chapter 2 of *Jane Eyre,* a classic of English literature by Charlotte Brontë first published in 1847. Your actor should read at least the relevant pages in order to enter young **Jane**'s world and engage with her plight. It is an important and mesmerising novel, and she may be motivated to read more.

Check that your actor has grasped the outline of Jane's situation: Jane came to live with Uncle Reed, her mother's brother, after the death of her own parents. Uncle Reed is now dead, and Jane is treated cruelly by her aunt, Mrs Reed, and her three cousins. Also among the household are Miss Abbott, the ladies' maid, and Bessie, the children's nursemaid. Mrs Reed has locked Jane in the red room as a punishment for attacking her cousin John (she was in fact defending herself against John).

> ### Project Work
>
> - CHARACTER WORKSHEET
> - KNOWLEDGE NOTES
> - STAGE DIAGRAM
> - OBSERVATION: *What happens in the body when you feel anger and fear*
> - ART: *The red room*
> - WRITING: *Why I attacked John*
> - GLOSSARY
>
> | | | |
> |---|---|---|
> | *orphan* | *closing in* | *endure* |
> | *flickering* | *pity* | |

Feelings: Anger and Fear

Jane is in a turmoil of anger and fear. The emotions wash over her in waves. Explore each feeling in turn.

Jane's Anger

The immediate sources of Jane's anger lie in the events leading up to this scene. With your actor, find points of focus for Jane's anger: these include the injustice of the punishment, the pain John has caused her and her rough handling by Bessie and Miss Abbott.

Delve further into Jane's history for deeper sources of anger: these include the death of her parents when she was very young, the death of Uncle Reed (whom she had become attached to), and years of feeling unwanted and unloved.

Now get Jane onto her feet to explore her anger. Remember to imbue these exercises with a sense of fun and play. Anger and fear are powerful emotions, and Jane's situation is upsetting. Finish off with something lighthearted (such as Jane's Revenge).

- GUESS HOW ANGRY I AM!

  First explore the feeling abstractly. (This is the emotional equivalent of stretching your muscles before playing sport.) Find a large cushion or beanbag and playing cards numbered 1–10. Ask your actor to think of something that would make Jane the tiniest bit angry (dropping her bookmark, for example) and to take that slight anger out on the cushion. That was level 1 on the anger scale, which goes up to 10. Find a level 10 situation, one that would cause Jane to feel incandescent rage, and ask her to take that out on the cushion. Encourage her to vocalise – by yelling, screaming, or shouting a word ('NO!!') or a phrase ('I don't believe it!!') This will help her to release the emotion through language (as she will when performing the scene).

For the game, the actor picks a card and immediately expresses anger at that level towards the cushion. Classmates guess her number. Encourage her to throw herself into the high numbers. Observe what happens in her body and face when she does.

Your actor might enjoy beating the hell out of your cushion, but stop if it becomes exhausting.

- **ANGRY JANE**
  Now go back to the list of sources for Jane's anger and bring them to life. You or classmates can stand in for John and the other cousins, Mrs Reed, her dead parents, and so on. Enact brief moments that cause the anger to well up in Jane. For example, John pulls Jane's hair and calls her 'Rat!'; or Jane's parents stand, hug Jane, push her away and fall to the floor, dead. Jane feels angry and takes it out on the cushion as before.

- **JANE IN THE RED ROOM**
  While the energy is up and the blood flowing, give Jane a go at the scene. Let her do it as she wants – loud, quiet, fast, slow, still or frantic – but challenge her to find moments to be angry at a level 9 or 10. Do it once through and move on. Store up any notes or direction for a future session.

- **JANE'S REVENGE**
  Finish up by giving Jane a chance to get her own back on the world. Repeat the Angry Jane exercise, but this time, instead of punching the cushion, she has a balloon with which to smash John, Mrs Reed, Bessie and so on. She can speak or shout or laugh as she's hitting back.

Jane's Fear

The entire sequence above can be repeated with the other emotion that drives Jane through this scene: fear. Identify causes of her fear. Then practise expressing different degrees of fear abstractly (a blanket will give her something to hug tight, or cover her head with, or crawl under). Next enact the things that frighten her so that she can express fear as a response. Finally give her a balloon and let her conquer her fears!

Follow-up

Give Jane highlighters or coloured pens. She chooses a colour for anger and a colour for fear and highlights or outlines portions of her script accordingly. She will see at a glance how she see-saws from one emotion to the other.

Further Ideas

- The geography of the red room is important; make sure Jane is clear about how it is laid out. Consolidate with a drawing or guided tour (see page 57).
- Create a spooky atmosphere in the rehearsal room. Turn the lights low and give torches and masks to classmates so that they can create shapes on the wall. Play eerie music.

THE STEPSISTER SPEAKS OUT
by Peg Kehret ✴ *Acting Anthology page 58*

Situation: The Story of Cinderella

Even if your students are familiar with Cinderella, a quick collaborative recap of the story will be useful and enjoyable. Any of these storytelling exercises will work well at the start of a class.

Project Work

- **CHARACTER WORKSHEET**
- **KNOWLEDGE NOTES**
- **STAGE DIAGRAM**
- **ART:** *Cinderella, warts and all*
- **WRITING:** *The real story of Cinderella*

GLOSSARY

stepsister	downright	designer label
bemoan	subsist	health club
good-natured	calories	caloric difference
sympathy	faithfully	chocolate éclair
nibble	perm	K-Mart
gnaw	facial	waltz
garbage	manicure	snag
coachman	Not on your life	

- Elicit from your student(s) the main details of the story: ask for the characters and then fill in the circumstances by asking leading questions, such as 'What are the differences between Cinderella and her stepsisters?', 'What big event is coming up?', and 'What magical things happen in the story?'

- Find (or create) a sequence of pictures that tells the story (examples can be downloaded from the web page which accompanies this book). Divide your class into teams and give each a jumbled set of illustrations and some blu-Tac. Teams race to stick the pictures on the wall in the correct order. Demonstrate the correct sequence to establish the story.
- The class retells the story (or part of it) one word at a time around the circle. Or a student tells a portion of the story and rolls a tennis ball to someone else when he wants to hand over.
- Retell the story in mime.
- In groups, act out the story in one minute. Then try to to do it in thirty seconds. Then ten seconds. Can they manage five seconds?!

Situation: A Different Point of View

With the traditional Cinderella storyline established, your actor should start trying to see events from her character's point of view. The way the story is usually told is completely wrong, and **Stepsister** wants to tell people what really happened. This is not about a downtrodden girl who got to be a princess but a little weirdo who got lucky.

- Come up with an alternative title for the story.
- Looking again at the sequence of pictures used earlier, Stepsister explains what is really going on in them. Encourage her to be hateful towards Cinderella.
- In a group, classmates act out short sequences from the story in silence. One group member, as narrator, gives the traditional telling in a sentence or two. The group repeats the sequence, but this time Stepsister, as narrator, gives her version of events.

- Look at the points of contrast between Cinderella and Stepsister in the build-up to the ball:

  Cinderella...
  - has a fairy godmother who turns pumpkins into coaches and turns rats into coachmen.
  - dusts, sweeps and sings.
  - makes a dress out of curtains.
  - dances with the prince.

  Stepsister...
  - does not have a fairy godmother.
  - eats pumpkin pie.
  - chases the rats away.
  - diets, exercises and has facials.
  - buys a fabulous gown.
  - dances with no-one.

- Choose a Cinderella and recreate a moment from the left column as a short mime. On the other side of the stage, Stepsister watches Cinderella then mimes the contrasting action from the right column. Cinderella is happy and enjoys herself; Stepsister is miserable.
- Return to the text and inject the scene with the resentment and envy that has built up during these exercises.

Situation: Imagined Audience

Where is Stepsister during this scene and who is she talking to? Might she be at the nail bar or the hairdressers? Or is she taking her complaint to the council of fairy godmothers?

Set up the chosen scenario with classmates. Whoever Cinderella is speaking to can make noises of assent and agreement ('oh, I know', 'yes, you're right') or noises of doubt and disagreement ('really?', 'that's not true') so that Stepsister has something to play off.

Decide what Stepsister wants from this conversation and what will be the outcome if she succeeds. She might want to persuade whoever she is talking to that she has been wronged. She might want the other person to feel indignation and outrage on her behalf. If she gets what she wants, Cinderella might suffer or be punished.

Take out the stand-ins and redo the scene. Can Stepsister play to the imagined scene partner with the same intensity and focus as she did to the real one?

✳ ACCENTS ✳

*R*eferences to garbage, pumpkin pie and K-Mart give this scene, like several in the Acting Anthology, an unmistakably American flavour.

As a rule, if a scene is obviously written for a particular accent, it should be done in the accent. The phrasing throughout this scene, ('Not on your life'; 'I never saw one yet who turned into a coachman') would not sound quite right in a British voice. However well acted, there is a risk that the performance will not ring true.

If your student cannot do a passable accent, choose a different scene. No examiner will expect perfection at lower grades, but a good approximation will demonstrate technical skill and engagement with the text.

When working with your student on an accent, focus on a few key sounds, repeated in the scene, that are pronounced differently from her home accent. Here, you might start with the vowel sound in 'ball'. Once she has learnt and practised a new vowel sound, she should look for all the words in the scene that contain it.

EVIL CAT
by Christina Kosaki ❋ *Acting Anthology page 59*

Physicality

Your actor will need to find a physicality that is somewhere between cat and human (see page 27). His instinct might be to crawl on all fours, but his performance will be hampered, and he will probably get sore knees. Establish from the outset that **Evil Cat** will walk on two legs. Ultra-realism is not the goal; this talking cat has plenty of human qualities. Nevertheless, he is a cat, not a human. What qualities of a cat's movement can your actor take on while remaining upright?

Project Work

- CHARACTER WORKSHEET
- KNOWLEDGE NOTES
- STAGE DIAGRAM
- RESEARCH: *Cats in motion*
- ART: *Floormap of the house*
- WRITING: *Bulletpoint plan for the day*

GLOSSARY

mobilize	stir	mercy
stroll	saunter	conquer
peer	kitty litter	big guns
contented	up to standard	toxic
thunk	have fire	guaranteed
rule with an iron paw		

There is plenty of research your actor can do, in class or at home. To start with, he should observe real cats in motion. If he has a cat at home, or if a friend or neighbour has one, ask him to record a short video of it doing something interesting. Otherwise, countless videos of cats are available on YouTube. (See page 9 for advice on working safely online.)

It might also be useful to observe how other actors have taken on the challenge of playing cats. A filmed version of the stage musical *Cats* is widely available. Various actors have played the comic-book hero/villain Catwoman. A good lead performance in *Puss in Boots* might offer ideas.

The cat behaviours your actor will need to mimic for this scene are:

- waking up
- padding around
- jumping
- scratching the litter
- picking at the carpet
- peering
- listening
- circling
- vomiting
- blinking.

❋ COMMAND GAMES ❋

A command game makes a good group warm-up. Students mill around the room (or enact a background situation); when you shout a command, they immediately perform the correct action or strike the correct pose.

Command games are simple and energetic and can be themed to suit whatever you are working on. Use them as an opportunity to practise physical acting by encouraging bold, strong movements. To make a command game competitive, award a point in each round for the most committed physical acting, or eliminate the student who does the correct movement last or does the wrong movement (see page 13 for notes on playing competitive games with youngsters). Include a release word (such as 'Prowl!') and a 'fall down dead' or 'go to sleep' command (here, 'Catnap!') to bring the game to a quiet, restful end.

GROUP GAME: CAT COMMANDS

Start by teaching the commands. You could use:

- Jump on the table!
- Scratch the litter!
- Miaow to the moon!
- Toxic vomit!
- Catnap!
- Stretch and wake up!

By choosing actions from the scene, you'll give Evil Cat some useful practice. If you have a group, ask your actor to watch his classmates. They might come up with ideas he could use in his performance.

Everyone moves around the room in a catlike way (they prowl, pad and peer). Shout a command. Once everyone has frozen in the correct pose or position, use a release word to return to general prowling. See the box opposite for suggestions on making a command game competitive.

Sequence of Actions

You could round off your work on the physical aspect of this scene by writing down and learning the sequence of actions. Then your actor can practise navigating through the scene using the actions alone without having to worry about his lines. The LAMDA examiner will ask him about his actions during the scene, so it is important to understand them clearly.

- You read the text, and your actor moves around the stage. Stop, start and repeat as you figure out together how the actions fit with the words.
- Read neutrally – if you act the scene, you'll be giving your student line readings and encouraging him to copy teacher instead of developing his own way of delivering the words.
- Work out the geography of the scene and map the route from hallway to bedroom to kitchen to bathroom.
- Consolidate: the actor moves silently through the whole sequence.
- Finally, the actor performs the sequence of actions with the words.

Further Ideas

VOICE

Find time during your work on Evil Cat's physicality to think about his voice. You could take the voice from the physicality and give it the same qualities – a voice can be as langourous, sleek, cunning or supercilious as a walk. Or you might look at the noises a cat really makes and identify English words that could be made catlike. You could miaow 'hours' and 'now', hiss 'sleep' and 'slaves' and purr 'stirring' and 'furry'.

STATUS

Characters have a status relationship with their surroundings as well as with other characters. Evil Cat has very high status in relation to this home and should walk around as if he owns the place and everything in it. He can even vandalise his surroundings, comfortable in the knowledge that his human slaves will repair the damage. Work on ways of expressing this high status. Does Evil Cat move slowly or quickly? With singular or multiple focus? How does he move his head?

WANTS

What does Evil Cat want? In what sense does he plan to take over the world?

Questing Knight

This scene has been adapted from a medieval romance, a type of poem that explores chivalry (what it means to be a good knight). Romances often feature knights going on quests and facing challenges that put their knightly qualities (such as courage and honour) to the test. **Gawain** jumps at the chance to demonstrate to King Arthur that he is a true knight by answering the Green Knight's challenge.

Gawain lives in a world of castles, maidens and fantastical creatures. Bring his world to life by asking your student (or your group) to design a quest that would challenge a knight. To succeed, the knight will need to be brave and honourable. Suggest that the quest include a journey, a time limit and something magical. If you want to give further help, cut up some pictures of typical Arthurian story elements, jumble them, and lay them out in a random order. Ask your students to construct a quest from the sequence. Alternatively, you could use fairytale-themed story dice.

Once the adventure has been mapped out, do an improvised staging of it with Gawain as the questing knight. Classmates can play the other roles.

Project Work

- CHARACTER WORKSHEET
- KNOWLEDGE NOTES
- STAGE DIAGRAM
- RESEARCH: *Medieval banquet halls*
- OUTING: *Manor house or castle*
- ART: *The Green Knight*
- WRITING: *Letter explaining where he is going (Green Chapel) and why*

GLOSSARY

challenge	confront	sarcastic
strike a blow	insult	remarkably
insolence	honour	sorcery

Feast Interrupted

Gawain launches into his speech with a strong reaction to the Green Knight. He is angry at the visitor's discourtesy, offended on behalf of his uncle (King Arthur) and eager to prove himself.

Help your actor to start with a bang by staging the build-up. Set up the room as a banqueting hall, with stand-ins (in a group class) for Arthur, the Green Knight and the feasting knights and ladies.

Students improvise a jolly Christmas feast. Once it is under way, the Green Knight thunders in and addresses the stunned diners scornfully. As he insult Arthurs and the knights, Gawain's fury builds. The Green Knight issues his challenge: is anyone bold enough to stand up and strike him – and be struck by him in return a year from now? Arthur leaps angrily to his feet, brandishing his axe. At that point Gawain, too, leaps up. Ask your actor to speak only the first three sentences. If necessary, go back and repeat until Gawain is performing those first sentences with appropriate intensity.

Medieval Banquet

Gawain has three points of focus: King Arthur, the Green Knight and his general audience – all the other feasters in the banqueting hall. If you are

❊ STAND-INS ❊

*I*f you have an hour-long class with six students doing six different scenes, it seems logical to give each student ten minutes each. If you do, every student spends fifty minutes twiddling thumbs. You could send them to a corner to learn lines or draw a picture, but that work could be done at home, and a drama class should be fun, active and energetic.

Involve students in one another's scenes. By giving the class a stake in all the performances, you'll foster a sense of group ownership and a supportive and collaborative atmosphere. When exam results come through, credit the whole group for individual successes.

Asking a student to take on the role of an unseen character in someone else's scene is of huge benefit to the main actor, but it's also an opportunity for the stander-in to stretch some acting muscles, free from pressure. Make sure he or she invests energy and thought in creating the other character. The more vivid and memorable those other characters are, the easier it is for the main actor to believe in them – and to convince his audience that they are there even after you have taken the stand-ins away.

The main actor must always be placed at the centre of the process and can veto anything that doesn't feel right. Don't allow a confident stander-in to dominate the scene. Their time will come! Their job for now is to provide the main actor with something to play off.

working in a group, it will be very useful to have stand-ins for the other characters. Help Gawain to decide where his focus switches. You could use these switches as a basis for any blocking or movement.

An online image search will help your student to build a clear picture of the setting. How large is the banquet hall, and how many people are in it? How is the shape and size of the setting reflected in the performance?

Character: Hotheaded Hero
Gawain is young (he has not yet had the chance to prove himself) and wants to show he is a man. He is proud and defiant, and his status is high, even in a room full of knights and a terrifying visitor. How does he stand, walk and turn?

Character: Gawain's Status
The higher Gawain's status is, the more dramatic the payoff when he watches, astounded, as the decapitated Green Knight rises to his feet and picks up his head. His status in relation to the Green Knight, whom he now calls 'sir', has nosedived. Is he frightened or just shocked?

If you have a stand-in for the Green Knight, you can make very good use of him. He and Gawain can script some lines and actions for the Green Knight. The staging and timing of the beheading and what comes after will need a lot of work, and a stand-in will be very helpful.

Further Ideas
- Draw the Green Knight.
- The fourteenth-century original will be impenetrable to your young actor, but if he is keen to read the whole story, Michael Morpurgo has written a modern-English children's version.

Jim's World

This scene has been adapted from a children's classic first published in 1883. This episode features in the sixth chapter, 'The Captain's Papers'. Your actor should have a go at reading the relevant chapter. He might be hooked enough to take on the whole novel. He could also watch one of the many film or TV adaptations.

Whether or not he does the background reading, your actor will need to step into the world of the story and grasp **Jim**'s situation. There are several ways you could help him:

- Read a vivid extract from the book (ideally from Chapter 6). At a suitable moment, pause and give him (and classmates) twenty seconds to make a tableau of the scene.
- Set quizzes (focus on Chapter 6). Tasks can include putting events in order, matching character to description and matching dialogue to character. A quiz can be downloaded from the web page which accompanies this book).
- Find published illustrations of the story or film stills and…
  - guess what is happening
  - put them in the order in which they occur in the story
  - create a tableau; bang a tambourine, and the tableau springs into life.

> ### Project Work
> - CHARACTER WORKSHEET
> - KNOWLEDGE NOTES
> - STAGE DIAGRAM
> - RESEARCH: *Treasure Island on film/TV*
> - ART: *Treasure map*
> - WRITING: *Script the whole scene*
> GLOSSARY
>
> | | | |
> |---|---|---|
> | coastal | ceremonious | account book |
> | widowed | sealed | latitude |
> | inn | fancy | longitude |
> | cursed | mate | sounding |
> | lodging | key | inlet |
> | oilskin | as like as not | anchorage |
> | squire | alter | bulk |

Excitement Builds

Jim is highly excited. Explore levels of excitement on a scale from 1 (mildly pleased) to 10 (ecstatic) using numbered cards. A student takes the stage, draws a card, looks at it and immediately says 'hooray!' Others guess his level.

Your actor can decide how excited Jim is at various moments and add numbers to his script. Alternatively, he can indicate excitement by colouring areas of the script (the brighter the colour, the more excited Jim is).

Jim starts the scene in a state of breathless excitement. Ask him to run around the hall or garden a few times, then burst onto the stage and begin.

Jim's Journey

The scene climaxes with Jim's discovery that he has found a treasure map. He proceeds to that realisation step by step, uncovering new pieces of information as though he were already hunting treasure. List each new discovery:

- There's something written in the middle.
- It says 'The Spyglass.'
- There are three red crosses.
- Two are in the north, one in the southwest.

> ### ✳ GUIDED TOURS ✳
>
> Scenes in the Acting Anthology are set in the past, present and future; all over the world and in other worlds; on land, at sea and in the air; indoors and outdoors; in tiny spaces and vast spaces; and in countless other locations both mundane and marvellous. The common factor is the blank stage. Your students have to imagine their setting, use the stage as though they are in the imaginary place and, when it comes to it, discuss their choices with the examiner.
>
> Students can design their stage by drawing, making a model (out of Lego, plasticine or craft materials) or using design software (see page 39). Ideas should be fixed with a stage diagram.
>
> Ask your students to present their stage design to you and classmates with a guided tour. They walk you around the stage and explain the location in as much detail as possible – not only where objects are placed but also where the scene's key events take place, environmental factors (weather, temperature, light) and what their attitude is to the setting. Prompt with questions, encouraging your actors to make choices where they haven't already.
>
> You can play as teacher and student or ask your actor to conduct the tour in character (so it comes closer to a hot-seating exercise – see pages 10 and 113). You and other tourists might also play in role. You might be viewing the location because you are considering coming to live there, because you are assessing it for health and safety or because you are a film location scout.

Does Jim's excitement build steadily or in leaps? Is he confused at any point?

Follow-up

In quiet time, your actor can draw the treasure map from Jim's description.

Unseen Characters

Script the whole scene, giving the other characters lines and actions. What can Jim deduce about the other characters' words and actions from the way he reacts? Classmates (if you have them) can stand in for the Maid, Dr Livesey and Squire Trelawney. Encourage full characterisations so that Jim has plenty to play off and can work out his different relationship with each of them.

Treasure Games

Work on Jim's feelings of suspense and discovery by playing a treasure game:

- **Where's the Treasure?**
  Send Jim out. Hide an item somewhere in the room. Jim returns and classmates whisper 'treasure, treasure'. They increase in volume the closer he gets to the treasure until he finds it. The treasure could be a final clue: write the location (eg, 'under the bin') in white crayon on white paper – the message is revealed by colouring the paper with a felt-tip pen.
- **Secret Finder**
  Send everyone out. Hide an item so that it is concealed but can be seen without moving anything. Students return and walk around. If a student sees the treasure, he does not react! He will give away its location. Instead he continues his walk, counting to ten silently in his head. When he reaches ten – and is away from the treasure – he sits down. Youngsters will need some practice at bottling their excitement. Not being able to let it out will focus them on how and where it is felt in the body.

Outdoor Adventure

Pippa lives in the moment, responding to the sights, sounds, smells and textures of the world around her and doing whatever it occurs to her to do next. If you have access to a garden or some outdoor space, stage an adventure to engage your actor with Pippa's state of wonder at her surroundings. A blindfold will heighten her senses.

Check that your actor knows what the five senses are. What happens to the other senses when you can't see? Explain that you want to 'turn up' her other senses by covering her eyes before taking her on a short outdoor adventure.

If you have a group, put your students into pairs. One is the adventurer, the other the guide. Adventurers are blindfolded, and guides keep them safe.

Once the adventurers are blindfolded, everyone stands in silence for a few moments. Give them time to relax and tune into the world around them. Direct them to foreground sounds (traffic, wind, birds) then ask them to listen deeper. Can they pick out quieter or more distant noises?

Guides stand in front of adventurers. The adventurer can hold the guide's elbow or hand. The guide walks very slowly around the space, being careful to avoid hazards (in a group, you'll need to monitor). The guide should lead the adventurer towards things that might smell or feel interesting.

It would be fun to include taste in this activity. Reassure students that they will get to taste something nice. Take careful note of dislikes, allergies and foods avoided. Place a bowl of chocolate buttons, digestive biscuits, raisins, or whatever you think appropriate somewhere in the space. Can adventurers work out what they tasted?

Round off by bringing everyone back together. Adventurers remove their blindfolds and describe their experience to you or the group.

If hands are dirty, give everyone a couple of minutes to clean up. If you have time, swap and repeat.

Project Work

- CHARACTER WORKSHEET
- KNOWLEDGE NOTES
- STAGE DIAGRAM
- OBSERVATION: *Heightened senses*
- OUTING: *Outdoor adventure*
- ART: *Scrap book; video diary*
- WRITING: *Adventure write-up*

GLOSSARY

reflect	*pass away*	*gunk*
mad about	*backside*	*finishing tape*
cobbled	*cowpat*	
foliage	*discus*	

Scrap Book

The source for this scene is a charming book by Clare and Michael Morpurgo. Try to get hold of a copy to show your actor. You could show it to her online (you can 'look inside' the book on the Amazon website).

The source is designed to look like Pippa's scrap book. Your actor can make a scrap book of her own. First, she will need to go on an adventure – during a trip to the countryside, around the school playground, in a local park or in her own back garden.

Although she must of course be supervised, it is important that she experience her outdoor adventure on her own. She should be free to interact with the environment without friends, brothers or pets to distract her. With no route planned, she should just go wherever her wellies take her – in her own private world, like Pippa.

Her scrap book could include at least a couple of paragraphs describing where she went, one drawing of herself, one drawing of something she saw and one foraged object.

Shared Experience

Who is Pippa talking to? This question does not have an obvious answer. However, this scene must have an outward focus or it will lack energy.

You could ask your actor to invent an imaginary companion for Pippa. Or she might be speaking to the world around her – the trees or the birds. Perhaps she is conversing with her wellies.

Pippa might be making a video diary or first-person documentary. Ask your actor to film her own outdoor adventure on her phone, narrating as she goes along, and to show the result to you or classmates in the next lesson.

Whatever choice you make, develop a relationship between Pippa and whoever or whatever she is speaking to. This is the first time Pippa has shared this experience. She guides and teaches enthusiastically as she goes along. What reaction would she like to get?

Group Game: What Are You Doing?

These are not recollected events. The scene is written in the present tense: Pippa commentates on her actions as she performs them. This quick non-competitive game – which finishes a class off nicely – plays on a similar idea.

The students line up. One (let's call him Yusuf) enters the playing space and mimes a simple action – brushing his teeth, for example. The next in line (let's call her Catherine) asks, 'What Are You Doing, Yusuf?' Yusuf answers with a completely different action: 'I'm riding a horse!' Catherine runs into the playing space, replacing Yusuf, and mimes the action he described (riding a horse). The next in line (Joshua) asks 'What are you doing, Catherine?' Her reply is again inaccurate: 'I'm popping balloons!' Joshua takes the space and mimes popping balloons.

Continue for as long as you want.

Further Ideas

- Discuss the likely springtime weather – wet, windy and quite warm. It is the beginning of May, and the English countryside is bursting with life.
- Practise aimless walking. First your actor crosses the space purposefully, as though she is a teacher hurrying to her next class or a mother going to pick her baby up from the crèche. Then she walks around, as Pippa does, with no particular sense of where she is going and no pressure of time. Switch from one to the other.
- Ask classmates to cheer Pippa on as she imagines racing to the finishing tape at the end of the scene.

Dalmatian Fur

Given this script, many actors (young and old) will leap to their feet and do a 'wicked stepmother' stereotype. Help your student to develop a richer performance by investigating what drives **Cruella de Vil** and what stands in her way (her wants and obstacles). The more decisions she makes, the more she will own her performance.

For Cruella, the idea of being dressed in Dalmatian fur is an all-consuming obsession. Everything about the way it feels and looks gives her intense pleasure, and she is deeply in love with herself clothed in white-with-black-spots. Cruella's obsession is no laughing matter. When she is not wearing Dalmatian fur, she feels incomplete.

> ### Project Work
> - CHARACTER WORKSHEET
> - KNOWLEDGE NOTES
> - STAGE DIAGRAM
> - RESEARCH: *Puppy behaviour*
> - ART: *Dalmatian designs; newspaper front page; Wanted poster*
> - WRITING: *Full scene*
>
> GLOSSARY
>
> | | |
> |---|---|
> | *dispose of* | *chloroform* |
> | *reversible* | *skinned* |

FUR DESIGNS

Engage your student with Cruella's obsession – and self-obsession – by asking her to design some Dalmatian fur items. She could create clothing, furnishings, accessories or whatever else comes to mind. Ask her to include herself in the pictures (for thoughts on drawing, see page 44).

If you have time, develop the exercise by asking Cruella to present her work. Create a scenario in which she has to 'sell' her designs – to fashion buyers, interior designers or shoppers. She should explain in detail the particular merits of Dalmatian fur.

THE PUPPIES

Once your actor has internalised Cruella's obsession with Dalmatian fur, ask her to imagine what thoughts run through Cruella's head when she looks at the puppies. She does not see adorable little creatures. She has no empathy for them. They exist to provide fur in much the way that an apple tree exists to provide apples. Their aliveness – the fact that they move around and make noise – is a huge irritation. It makes them hard to keep track of and increases the danger that they will be found.

Make sure the puppies are present in the scene. Find moments for Cruella to interact with them. Imagine their actions towards her and her responses.

Cruella imagines killing the puppies as a delightful experience, something she would do expertly in all sorts of lovely ways. Is this simply sadism? Or does her pleasure derive from the excitement of having all that Dalmatian skin suddenly available to use? Does it derive from being rid at last of the scampering, barking pests? Whatever choice you make will give her cruelty a root and take your actor's performance away from pantomime villainess.

The dilemma Cruella faces is that the apples are not yet ripe. If she kills the puppies now, the skins will not be big enough for all the items she wants to make from them. If your actor feels Cruella's frustration at this situation, her snappiness and her scornfulness will have an emotional root.

Cruella Under Pressure

There is plenty of jeopardy in this scene. Cruella would like to wait until the puppies are bigger, but there is a real threat that her stolen Dalmatians will be tracked down and the whole scheme ruined. Remember how badly she wants her fur, even in a reduced quantity. Time is running out.

To make matters worse, Cruella's accomplices are more of a hindrance than a help. Although they have some use as henchmen, they are dim-witted and lazy and do not share Cruella's feelings about Dalmatian fur. The more you set them up as obstacles stopping Cruella getting what she wants, the greater the dramatic impetus the scene will have.

Context

The source is the twelfth chapter (called 'Sudden Danger') of Dodie Smith's 1956 children's novel. Your student will deepen her understanding of the context by reading the relevant chapter. Most Grade 2 actors should find the whole book manageable. In the exam, your actor will be asked where the scene is located, so spend time deciding exactly what this room looks like and mapping out the stage (see page 57).

A nice homework or quiet-corner task for your actor would be to draw the front page of one of the newspapers Cruella refers to. Or she might draw a Wanted poster. You could improvise a televised appeal from the Dearlys or a chat-show interview in which they talk about their sadness and loss.

Your actor will very likely have seen either the animated or the live-action Disney film. Suggest that she does not watch it again while preparing this scene. The examiner will want to see her version of Cruella de Vil, not a copy of Glenn Close's or the one created by the animators. What does Cruella look like in your actor's imagination?

Saul and Jasper

If you have a group, time invested early on in creating Saul and Jasper and inserting them into the scene will reap dividends in later rehearsals when you take them out. Ask your actor to expand the scene to a full script that includes the unseen characters. Write their lines and their stage directions. Place them on stage in such a way that Cruella can address them and still face front. Plan with her who she is talking to at each point.

Encourage the supporting actors to invest in their characters' physicality and to commit to their reactions, so that Cruella always has something to bounce off (see the note on stand-ins on page 55.)

Pay particular attention to the opening (a golden rule for any piece of solo acting). In the novel, Cruella flings the door open and sees Saul and Jasper dozing in front of the television. A dramatic entrance would launch this scene nicely. Explore the contrast between her state of mind and theirs to heighten the intensity of the first lines.

EVACUEE
by Jenny Thornton ❋ *Acting Anthology page 69*

Evacuees

Evacuation is a good subject for your young actor to research. A list of accessible and appropriate resources can be downloaded from the web page which accompanies this book.

    Encourage your student to imagine what it would be like to be an evacuee.

- If we were a family living in London in 1939, and we found out you had to be evacuated, what would happen to you?
- Who would go with you?
- Where would you go? What would the journey be like?
- Who would be there?
- How long would you be there for?
- Would you be safer? Would you be happier?
- If I gave you half an hour to pack, what would you take with you?

Was it a good idea to evacuate children? If there is disagreement among group members, stage a debate. You could be in role as a London father, with classmates as children. Some try to convince you to evacuate them, and others try to convince you not to.

    If your students could pack only one item, what would they choose? Place an imaginary suitcase in the centre of the room. Each student in turn mimes looking through her belongings before selecting one item and putting it in the case. Alternatively, play 'I went to the countryside and I took…' Each student names all the previous items and adds one of her own.

> ## Project Work
> - CHARACTER WORKSHEET
> - KNOWLEDGE NOTES
> - STAGE DIAGRAM
> - RESEARCH: Evacuation and evacuees
> - OUTING: Second World War museum
> - WRITING: Diary of first day as an evacuee
>
> GLOSSARY
> air raid   gas mask   parlour
> mac   curlers

❋ SPEAKING TO THE AUDIENCE ❋

Several solo scenes in the Acting Anthology are addressed 'to the audience'. This convention usually means that a character is narrating events or expressing thoughts aloud.

    When addressing the audience, it is best that your actor does not eyeball the examiner. Seeing the examiner periodically look down from the stage to write notes (as they all must do) might cause your student to lose focus. There is no examiner present in the imaginary situation, and direct eye contact will make it difficult for an actor to sustain the illusion and difficult for an examiner to suspend disbelief and engage with the actor's imagined world. Give your students practice at playing to either side of the examiner and above the examiner's head.

    Deciding that a character is just 'thinking aloud' tends to make solo scenes airy and uninteresting. Your actor should make a specific choice about who these thoughts are being shared with. An imaginary friend? God? A dead relative? Her younger self? If she has a relationship with whoever she is addressing, she can add intention to what she is saying and think about the effect she would like her words to have.

Period photographs of evacuees will stimulate valuable work. You might ask groups to choose a photograph and make a tableau imitating it. Tap a student to unfreeze her and ask who she is and how she is feeling. Or let the group decide their situation together. At your signal, the photo comes to life.

Location

This scene has several locations:

- **Paulette**'s home
- The journey to the station
- The platform in London
- The train
- The platform in the countryside
- Mrs Smith's house (maybe)

Spend some time with your actor working out what each location looks like. You could incorporate research by looking at period photographs.

Ask your student to take the stage and place her (or him – a boy could play this as Paul) in each location in turn. Ask her what is around her. How familiar is this location to her? How long will she spend there? Who is close by? How does she feel in this location?

Test how well she understands and communicates each location with a quick game: ask her to pick one of her locations and stand or walk in it. Can you or her classmates guess from her body language where she is?

Work on the transitions from one location to another. A fluid scene would give the sense that Paulette is whisked from place to place. Juddering transitions would allow your actor to express the sharp shocks of her journey. A large playing space will allow you to set each location on a different area of the stage. If you are using chairs, your actor might set the stage up before beginning her performance. Or a single chair might be moved as required during the performance.

Make sure that your student has securely grasped all your work on location so that she can discuss her choices in her exam.

Who Is Paulette?

We know from the text that Paulette is a young girl with a mother. She cries when she is unhappy. She loves her home and has never seen the countryside. She finds Mrs Smith fierce. Beyond this, your student is free to invent details of Paulette's life. She might work entirely from her imagination. She might base Paulette on a character from a book or a real evacuee she has researched. A thorough back story will mean a richer, fully owned performance.

Unseen Characters

Engage classmates to play Mum, the guard and Mrs. Smith. It will be valuable for Paulette to try the central conversation as dialogue with a student (or you) in the role of Mum.

The opening line of the scene is a reaction. Has Mum just asked Paulette to pack her suitcase? Whatever you decide, stage the run-up to the opening so that Paulette can practise starting strongly.

Encourage your stand-in actors to give committed performances so that Paulette has plenty of ideas when it comes to developing and playing the other characters herself.

A TOUCH OF GOLD

adapted by LAMDA from an ancient Greek myth ✳ Acting Anthology page 71

Starter: One Wish

Ask your actor what he would wish for if he could have one wish. (Outlaw wishing for more wishes!) In a group, go around the circle. You might step into role as a genie or fairy godmother.

From a group, you will probably get a mix of selfish and altruistic wishes. Ask each student to come up with one wish for themselves and one wish for other people or the world. Ask what might be the pitfalls of some of the wishes. The conversation can lead to King **Midas**, whose selfish wish brings him disaster and heartbreak.

Project Work

- CHARACTER WORKSHEET
- KNOWLEDGE NOTES
- STAGE DIAGRAM
- RESEARCH: Midas story
- ART: Garden of statues
- WRITING: Letter to gods requesting cancellation of golden touch

GLOSSARY

immense	snoop	regret
grant	short-staffed	gold leaf
consequence	goblet	hound
rumour	empire	lyre

Ten-Second Statues

Students pick a human or animal character and move around the space without bumping into one another. At your signal, they have been touched by King Midas. As you count slowly to ten, they turn into golden statues.

Explore the transformation with your students. The whole body might slowly seize up as one. Or the body might seize up limb by limb. Whichever they choose will give good practice at body control.

When everyone is frozen, announce that you are King Sadim and that you have the un-golden touch. Over another slow count of ten they regain movement until they can move freely around the space as before.

Some suitable background music will help your students to focus on their physicality during this exercise. Ballet music is always a good bet; see page 107 for reflections on using music in drama classes.

Realisation Dawns

Ask your actor or group how Midas felt when he first found out he had the golden touch (astonished, thrilled) and how he felt after he froze his daughter (shocked, miserable). They're going to practise the change from one emotion to the other.

Put students into pairs: one is Midas, the other is his dog, Hellen. Midas has just been told his wish has been granted. Hellen comes running up to him. On your signal, he pats her or hugs her, and she slowly turns to gold. A golden dog! At first he watches, delighted. Then, when she is completely frozen, he gradually realises (over another count to ten) that Hellen will never again run up to him in the garden.

If your students are managing the slow transitions well, don't count. Alternatively, count when they are working as a group and then invite pairs to show their short scene to the class without you counting.

✳ CIRCLE TIME ✳

*I*t is a good idea to start a drama class with circle time. Sitting in a circle together gives young students a chance to adjust their energy to a suitable level and switch their focus to the class. Play a quick game to help this process – something mental rather than physical, and cooperative rather than competitive. For a list of suggestions, see the web page which accompanies this book.

Make sure everyone contributes to your conversation. Be prepared to keep a hand on the steering wheel. The most important skill to foster in circle time is not speaking but listening. A reluctant speaker will remain reluctant if he is forever interrupted or ignored. Conversely, being listened to by you and peers will boost his confidence.

Listen carefully yourself and round off circle time with a quiz: 'Rhiannon, what's Andrei's favourite ice cream?' 'Jaspal, what would Alice's dream holiday be?' Give lots of praise for correct answers. Remind your students that a good actor is a good listener.

Character: Midas and Jason

On the one hand, Midas is the king in his palace, and Jason is just a boy from the village. On the other, the king shows Jason around, confides in him and doesn't seem to want him to leave. Work with your actor on Midas' relationship with Jason. Who is this boy? What does he look like? Is he confident or nervous in the king's company? Does he remind the king of anyone else he knows? Does Midas enjoy the company of children?

Engage a classmate, if you have one, in the process of creating a character for Jason. Rehearse the scene with a stand-in Jason; establish Jason's actions and reactions, so that Midas has plenty to play off. In the exam, Midas will be asked about his actions during the scene. Therefore, it is crucial that he understands what he says and does to Jason. What does Midas want from the young villager?

Game: Don't Touch Me!

Jason decides to stay in Midas' company but must avoid being touched by him. Explore this dynamic with a Midas-themed game.

Students form a large circle. One (let's call him Michael) stands centre. He has the golden touch. He walks slowly towards a student in the circle (Dorina), his hands outstretched. Dorina must be rescued before Michael reaches her, or she'll be a statue and out of the game. She chooses someone else in the circle: 'Help me, Gabriel!' When Gabriel replies, 'Come here, Dorina', she is released. The golden touch transfers to Dorina. Michael takes Dorina's place as she walks towards Gabriel, hands outstretched. Now Gabriel must ask for help.

When your students have a healthy fear of the golden touch, an improvisation will help you to stage the last portion of the scene. Midas shows Jason around his palace gardens. Midas has the golden touch, so Jason must avoid touching him. But Midas is the king, so Jason must be careful not to speak out of turn or do anything to offend him.

Further Idea

Tell (don't read) the whole story of King Midas and the Golden Touch. A text is available on the web page which accompanies this book.

Should I or Shouldn't I?

Bobby is reluctant to confide in Peggy, and his inner turmoil sets the tone of this scene's opening. You could start the class with a general discussion about the rights and wrongs of 'telling on' people. Then talk about Bobby's particular situation. Make a list of the pros and cons (for Bobby) of sharing his secret with his sister.

Next play the very opening of the scene, as far as the fiddling with the Latin book. After 'What is wrong?', Bobby pauses, and classmates (or you) whisper arguments for and against spilling the beans. Bobby considers the arguments as he speaks the next words, pausing as he tussles with his conscience. Finally, he makes the decision: 'if you really want to know ….'

Try without the thoughts being whispered aloud; ask Bobby to hear the voices in his head as he struggles to make up his mind. Can he hear the voices again when he repeats two of the arguments ('I hate to be a sneak'/'you are my sister')?

Justice and Injustice

Bobby takes his punishment and is determined to get revenge as soon as he is big enough. He is tough, but in the absence of Archie (an older friend who has gone away to school elsewhere), he doesn't have an ally to champion him. Telling a teacher is not an option for Bobby – why? Would your actor's response to being bullied be similar to or different from Bobby's?

At the end of the scene, Bobby finds reasons to be cheerful – his beatings are not as bad as those some other boys receive, and the thought of Peggy beating up Jones Minor makes him smile and laugh.

GAME: UNFORTUNATELY/FORTUNATELY

This quick game will take your actor into the mindset of someone determined to find the upside of things. Starting with the word 'Unfortunately', offer a situation that looks bad: 'Unfortunately, there is a nasty bully in the school.' He answers back with a positive perspective: 'Fortunately he leaves me alone' or 'Fortunately he was abducted by aliens.' Continue back and forth a few times.

The injustice of his situation angers Bobby, and the thought of justice being done pleases him. Your actor can use his 'Fortunately's to right some wrongs.

Now ask Bobby to retell the sequence. Encourage him to feel dejected by the unfortunate events before cheering himself up with a sunny thought.

This game works well in a group – go around the circle in turn, building a story that see-saws between glum and cheery outlooks.

Project Work

- CHARACTER WORKSHEET
- KNOWLEDGE NOTES
- STAGE DIAGRAM
- RESEARCH: Pony trap
- OBSERVATION: Bumpy ride
- ART: Jones Minor

GLOSSARY

accustomed	confidence	fellow
account	forthcoming	buckle-strap
doings	dog-eared	champion
scarcely	breathe a word	lavatory basin
flustered	sneak	sparring-cock
laugh it off		

Actions: What Happened?

Bobby is recalling past events, so there is no direct action in this scene. He is in a pony trap and would be seated. Nevertheless, there are opportunities for movement and action. It is important to make the most of them, since Bobby will be asked about his actions (what he did and why) in his exam. Bobby might, for example, get into the trap at the top of the scene and out again at the end. He will need to find a way of communicating the movement of the trap throughout the scene, by swaying or jiggling. You might find a moment or two when one of the trap's wheels hits a bump.

VIVID RECOLLECTION

Bobby might also become very animated as he recalls being pulled, twisted and hammered. If he has a vivid picture of being beaten up by Jones Minor, he can relive the events he is describing.

Ask your actor to work out exactly what happened between leaving school and arriving at the meeting place with Peggy. Recruit a classmate to play Jones Minor. Give the pair some time to work on staging the fight. In a one-on-one class, either you will have to step in as Jones Minor or the other character can be imagined. Draw attention to Bobby's suffering; pause during each bit of punishment, and ask Bobby which part of his body hurts. How does he feel? Afraid? Angry? Close to tears? How long ago was he supposed to meet his sister? Does he want to escape? What will make Jones Minor stop?

Immediately play the portion of the scene in which Bobby recalls the beating. Allow him to use the whole stage. Ask him to act out what happened as he describes it, using lots of energy.

Repeat, but this time confine him to a small part of the stage. Ask for the same energy and commitment. Try a third time with Bobby seated – and decide whether he should remain seated throughout or might get to his feet.

If you have time, stage the other beatings Bobby recalls.

Location

Your actor can get a sense of the location by looking at period photographs (try an image search for 'pony trap turn of the century') or watching clips of movies or TV series set in rural England around 1900. If he has any opportunity to take a ride in a trap, a cart or anything jerky or bumpy, he can observe how his body is moved around.

Source Text

This scene has been adapted from a 1904 children's novel. The conversation between Bobby and Peggy can be found in Chapter 19, called 'Peggy at War'.

For the modern reader, some of the social attitudes in the book seem offensively snobbish. In the fifth chapter there is a parody of a slave song which includes terminology now considered racist. Whatever the rights and wrongs of applying twenty-first-century judgements to Victorian attitudes, this is not a book we would encourage young students to read.

Chapter 19 is fairly unobjectionable, and it rounds off this episode. If your student is keen to find out whether Jones Minor gets his comeuppance, print or copy the relevant pages.

Courage Under Fire

Examine how the characters respond to their perilous situation. Faced with imminent death and in a lot of pain, **Darktan** is grimly courageous. **Nourishing** is flustered but gathers her wits and searches for a solution. She shows obedience, knowledge and initiative. It is important to Darktan that both rats prevent emotion from clouding judgement; they must 'keep calm and carry on.' These exercises and games will embed some of these characteristics:

> ### Project Work
> - CHARACTER WORKSHEET
> - KNOWLEDGE NOTES
> - STAGE DIAGRAM
> - RESEARCH: Rats in motion
> - ART: Keep Calm poster; location of scene; celebratory front page
> - WRITING: Mission outline
>
> GLOSSARY
>
> rodent   disposal   grind
>
> plague   sarcasm

- KEEP CALM AND . . .
  Variations on this message are found on water bottles, pencil cases and lunchboxes, and your actors are likely to have come across it. Ask them to design a 'Keep Calm' poster with a motto their character might live by.
- UNDRAMATIC DYING
  Dramatic dying can be woven into any number of games. Reverse the challenge so that the actor is in extreme pain but must struggle not to show it. Encourage exaggeration – you want to see the struggle. If it helps, suggest gruesome deaths (all the blood in your body turns to acid; a million needles prick your skin; you are tied down and tickled to death).
- THINKING QUICKLY
  Gather a collection of random props, and give your two actors a perilous situation to improvise (they are hanging from a cliff edge; a zombie army is advancing up the alleyway). Their job is to find a way out of the situation. Once they get going, throw a prop onto the stage. They must use it to solve their dilemma. Extend the scene by throwing in more props.

Rats Underground

What words spring to mind when your actors think of rats? These might describe movement (scurrying, scuffling), physicality (sleek, quick), behaviour (twitching, gnawing) or personality (cunning, alert). Can they incorporate ratlike qualities into the way they move around the stage?

The scene is set in a tunnel, but your actors are free to decide what kind of a tunnel – large or small, damp or dry, rock or earth. Ensure they make clear decisions. A drawing of the setting will help crystallise those decisions.

Two Heads Are Better Than One

What do the two characters want from each other? Darktan wants Nourishing to follow his example. Nourishing wants to win praise (or promotion) from Darktan. What reaction is Nourishing seeking when she points out for the second time that she gnawed through the spring on the trap?

❋ STAGE DIRECTIONS ❋

This scene has been extracted from a stage play, and stage directions have been imported along with dialogue. The writer did not envisage a performance under exam conditions. Stage directions specify a follow spot, wings, a grinding sound and a blackout.

Nobody will be operating a follow spot or a sound desk during a LAMDA exam. As for wings, putting Darktan offstage would prevent your actor from sharing his performance with the examiner. Miming the trap in full sight allows him to demonstrate his skill. Ignore stage directions that do not support your goal – to help your students to meet the assessment criteria.

Some dramatists write good stage directions that help actors find ways of playing a scene. 'Dreamily' may be the perfect way to say 'Quite nice, really.' Investigate the moment and find out for yourselves. If dreamy doesn't work, find an alternative that does. The same applies to actions. The dramatist may have chosen the perfect moment for a character to jump, laugh or shudder. However, if an action doesn't work, don't do it. Truthfulness is the bottom line.

When preparing clean copies of scenes (Acting Anthology and own-choice) for the exam, leave out the stage directions. They clutter up the page and make it harder for the examiner to keep track of the lines while watching the performance.

Both also want to succeed in their mission – to find and destroy traps. How do they complement each other? Could either succeed by working alone?

Source Text

Reading the play from which this scene is extracted will give your students some background on their characters and the story leading up to the scene. However, the scene speaks for itself: the characterisation is strong, and the situation is well described. It might be useful to know that just before this episode, Darktan has escaped from a fighting pit, where he outwitted and wounded a dog the cruel ratcatchers forced him to fight. Though either character could be played by either gender, in the original Darktan is male and Nourishing is female.

The play is adapted from the novel by Terry Pratchett (this episode appears in Chapter 9). The adaptation is reasonably loose, and though it's an enjoyable read, the novel is not essential background reading.

The Stakes Are High

High stakes are crucial for any drama, especially when you have only two minutes to tell a story. If there is nothing at stake, the story falls flat. Think in terms of jeopardy. What are the chances and consequences of failure?

Hot-seat your actors to embed the idea that their mission places them in grave danger. You could step into role as their military commander. Check their understanding of the task they face by asking them for a run-down of the plan and the dangers they must avoid. Or set it up as a TV interview. The interview could take place after the events of the scene, with you as the interviewer celebrating the rats' heroic courage and cunning. Your students could follow up by designing a newspaper front page glorifying Darktan and Nourishing.

Break It Up

Help your actors to break the scene up into chapters. A new chapter begins when the scene turns in a different direction because something significant happens or because the conversation changes subject. A chapter might last a whole page or a couple of lines.

Look at the opening lines. Where do your actors detect the first significant shift in the scene? One answer would be that it comes halfway through **Goalie**'s fourth line: 'You know it wasn't' continues the argument about the ref's decision, whereas 'If you score now…' shifts the focus to the penalty itself. Goalie has accepted that protesting is pointless: the penalty decision is final.

What names could you give the first two chapters? The opening might be 'Yes Ref, No Ref!' The second one might be 'Goalie Feels Wronged.'

Breaking the script up into chapters can give clues about blocking. A possible first move is given in the stage directions – both players are getting up. In the twelfth line, **Striker** tells Goalie to get back on his (or her) line. So somewhere in between, Goalie has walked to his line and stood ready to face the penalty. The turning point from the first to the second chapter would be the best place for this move. Break up the whole scene in this way.

> ## Project Work
> - CHARACTER WORKSHEET
> - KNOWLEDGE NOTES
> - STAGE DIAGRAM
> - OUTING: *Sunday football match*
> - ART: *Comic strip of scene*
> - WRITING: *Letter to referee protesting the red card*
>
> GLOSSARY
>
> | | | |
> |---|---|---|
> | clash | hot shot | peg-leg |
> | travesty | cocky | divot |
> | shin | abandon | |

The Referee

The referee often drives the action. It is his (or her) whistle blow which kickstarts the scene, and it is his showing of the red card to both players that carries the scene to its conclusion. His warnings, decisions and commands continually affect both players. They appeal to him, plead with him and berate him throughout.

Therefore, your two actors must have a clear and strong sense at all moments of exactly where Ref is and what he is doing.

The most helpful way of giving the referee solidity is to rehearse the scene with an actor standing in. Direct and block the referee, giving his actions and decisions strong definition. You might give him a few short lines, but he could probably work through the scene using only his whistle and strong gestures See page 55 for thoughts on using stand-ins.

You'll need the referee standing downstage of the players, facing up, so that when they address him in their exam performance, they face front.

Only take Ref out of the scene when you're sure that his performance is fixed in Goalie's and Striker's mind. Test the actors by stopping the scene and asking them to close their eyes and point at the referee's face. When they open their eyes again, are they both pointing at the same spot?

The Tussle

Towards the end of the scene, the players 'clash and roll around the floor.' Make sure you set aside some time to work on this little piece of action. Your actors' safety is paramount; at no point should there be hard contact with the floor or each other. Any tussle should be well rehearsed. The actors should be fully in control of their bodies, and each should know precisely what the other is doing.

A fundamental principle of stage combat is 'actors working together, characters in opposition.' Give your actors practice at the three steps of combat: (i) positions; (ii) eye contact; (iii) action. It is crucial that they make eye contact before launching into anything physical.

Set your actors the difficult challenge of 'selling' the fight. They must show agressive intent on their faces while being soft in their hands and arms. The noises they make (howls, grunts and shrieks) will also convince an audience that they are really going for each other.

A simple and safe way of getting your actors onto the floor is for one to push the other (gently) between the shoulder blades; the pushed actor then lunges forward with one foot and puts his hands on the floor in a press-up position before flattening himself. At speed and with the right expression and sound, this will convince as a fall.

Further Ideas

CHARACTERS

The writer has not provided biographical details for the two characters. Encourage your actors to take ownership by creating full back stories for Striker and Goalie. Fill in character worksheets, which can be downloaded from the web page which accompanies this book; draw pictures; put characters in the hot seat. Have these characters met before this football match? How are they different from each other? Which is the bossier? The smarter? The more short-tempered?

OVERLAPS

An actor should know what he was going to say before he was cut off, otherwise the effect is unconvincing. 'But you —'.

❋ LEARNING LINES (2) ❋

Remind your students to learn not only their lines but also their cues. Being sharp on your cues is vital for pace and energy. A scene in which cues are not picked up sags; a scene in which the actors are really tight on their cues is exhilarating to watch (and perform). A pause between one line and the next must be a matter of choice.

Help your actors to embed their cues:

• In rehearsal, ask an actor to repeat the last word or phrase of the other actor's line before beginning his own.

• Test actors on their cues. One actor reads only his cues; the other responds with full lines. They switch. When they think they really know their lines, throw cues at them out of order and see if they can give the right line in response.

• Maybe your actor's real cue – the word that sparks his next thought – is not the last word the other actor says, but a word a little further back. Find the word that triggers his reaction.

'How can you stand there and —'. These and other unfinished sentences must be completed by the actors. They should learn the full sentence and make as if to say it, so that the other actor really does interrupt them.

UNICORNS AND ALLEY CATS

by D M Larson ✻ *Acting Anthology page 83*

Animal Characters

Performing on hands and knees is not a good idea, so your actors' challenge is to bring a catlike or unicornish quality to upright movement. **Dude** will find plenty of videos of cats online (bear in mind the note on internet safety on page 9). He should research ways a cat moves when it is in its home environment. **Kim** could base her physicality on a horse or zebra. What refinement might she introduce to suggest a unicorn? They are often drawn with long eyelashes and large soft eyes. Could her movement have a dreamy quality?

There are other cats and horses in the Acting Anthology, so look for opportunities for students to work together on their animal characters.

Another approach would be to ask Dude and Kim what body part they are led by (where is their character's physical centre?) First they move around the room in neutral. Then they experiment with different body parts leading them forward – Kim could try knees, eyes or nose (horn); Dude could try ears, teeth or tummy. For more on animal characters, see page 27.

Project Work

- CHARACTER WORKSHEET
- KNOWLEDGE NOTES
- STAGE DIAGRAM
- RESEARCH: Cats and horses
- OBSERVATION: Feeling at home / like a fish out of water
- OUTING: City on a rainy night
- ART: Dude's alley; Jagged Peaks
- WRITING: Postcard home (Kim); poem about the city (Dude)

GLOSSARY

dweller	startled	shudder
bustle	awe	distaste
unequalled	on guard	respond
yowl	crush	frustration
slam on the brakes		

City and Country

How does life in the city differ from life in the country? Ask for pairs of opposite adjectives: the city is noisy, always moving and dangerous, whereas the country is calm, still and peaceful. These adjectives might also describe the characters of city-dwelling Dude and country-dwelling Kim.

Find music or a soundscape which evokes the rhythms of the city at night – upbeat, chaotic, menacing – and ask your Dude actor to move around the room as though he is prowling his streets. The sounds can guide his movements. Give him some of his lines to speak and ask him to match the volume, pace and tone of the soundtrack.

Switch your actors and play a rural soundscape or piece of music. In the same way, allow your Kim actor to find her own 'home rhythm' as well as her natural voice. Now challenge her to maintain the same rhythm to the urban soundtrack. Can she feel how it jars?

Finally, play the whole scene against the urban soundtrack. Find a volume level which Dude can speak over comfortably but which forces Kim to raise her voice above her natural volume. Play it again with no noisy background – can your actors imagine the city din?

Status in the Space

Dude is comfortable in his alley. He is at home and in charge. If danger arises, he knows the ways in and out. Kim is uncomfortable, lost and confused. She is powerless and doesn't know how she would escape if things were to become dangerous. His status in relation to the space is high; hers is low.

Status in the space (how comfortable a person feels in his or her surroundings) can have a dramatic effect on body language. Explore this by playing a simple scenario and altering the circumstances:

- An actor sits in a chair as though she is watching TV.
- In the first scenario, she is watching TV in her favourite chair at home.
- In the second, this is her first visit to a new piano teacher. Her Mum has dropped her off and left. The teacher has asked her to wait in the dining room while she finishes her previous class in the next room. The TV is on.

Your actor's body language switches from relaxed to tense. Why? In the first scenario, she is comfortable in the space. Everything is familiar. She knows where things are and how they work. If she wants to switch channels, turn a light on or eat an apple, she can. In the second, everything is unfamiliar. The sounds and smells are strange. She is powerless to do anything except wait.

Dude's situation matches the first scenario – his body language should be open and relaxed. Kim's matches the second – she is tense and wary.

SETTING

The location is Dude's domain, so your actor can design the space to suit a cat perfectly. It could be an awkward place for a unicorn to end up, with places where hooves might easily become wedged or a horn trapped. Dude can share his ideas by leading a guided tour (see page 57).

Relationship

For much of the scene Kim is miserable and homesick, and Dude's attempts to cheer her up do not seem to work. When he leaves, she 'looks around sadly at the city'. Then she suddenly brightens, splashes playfully through the puddles and skips off happily. What has cheered her up?

If Kim's happiness were placed on a scale from 0 (deeply unhappy) to 10 (overjoyed), where do your actors think she is at the end of a scene? How does she get there? Does she leap through the numbers in that final brief moment or does her mood gradually lift? Play through the scene and look for points where Kim feels sparks of happiness. Add numbers to the script.

What does Dude want out of this situation? How does he feel when Kim is negative about his alley? Or when she says she feels better? Exploring the complex relationship between Dude and Kim will help your actors to talk in their exam about their actions in the scene (what they do and why they do it).

Break It Up

If your actors divide this scene into chapters, they will get a clearer picture of the emotional journey Dude and Kim take through the scene and of the key turning points. Give the chapters names that include one or both characters' names ('Dude's Love Song to the City' or 'Kim's Big Regret', for example).

Source

This scene is adapted from a classic of American children's literature, written in 1913. The scene closely matches its original, described in Chapter XI ('Introducing Jimmy'). If she reads it, **Pollyanna** will learn about Aunt Polly, Fluffy and Buffy and the Ladies' Aid.

The source provides a location: a roadside in Vermont, where Pollyanna comes across a 'disconsolate little heap' one pleasant Thursday morning.

Gladness

The book was so popular that the idea of a young girl who makes it her job to spread gladness (cheer people up)

became widely known. The word 'Pollyanna' entered the language as a description of anyone who (like Porter's character) has a sunny disposition and a sympathetic soul. When confronted with the taciturn **Jimmy Bean**, Pollyanna knows that cheering him up will be a challenge. Is it one that she relishes? Has she ever failed in her mission to spread gladness?

Project Work
- CHARACTER WORKSHEET
- KNOWLEDGE NOTES
- STAGE DIAGRAM
- RESEARCH: *Orphans*
- ART: *Orphanage; disconsolate heap*
- WRITING: *Diary of today's events; wish list; letter to local residents*

GLOSSARY

orphan	whittle	Ladies' Aid
stern	hesitate	abrupt
philosophy of life	huntin' up	dawning
positive effect	scornful	critical
calf's foot jelly	goin' on	presence
restless	Matron	

Yin and Yang

The initial contrast between Pollyanna and Jimmy Bean should be stark. The more glum he is, the richer the payoff when she prods a reaction out of him.

Explore this contrast with a game of Fortunately/Unfortunately. Your actors tell a story in turn, one sentence at a time. Pollyanna starts by describing a happy situation, beginning with the word 'Fortunately.' Jimmy Bean, seeing the downside, counters with 'Unfortunately...'. She finds the silver lining; he casts a cloud, and so on. Encourage bold ideas and challenge Pollyanna to make Jimmy Bean smile at the resilience of her optimism.

Why the Long Face?

Jimmy Bean is dejected because he felt unwanted at the overcrowded Orphans' Home. This experience is central to his mood in the scene. If it is vivid in your actor's mind, he will be able to 'recall' it. Neither this scene nor the original novel offer much more in the way of a background for Jimmy Bean, so your actor is free to invent his back story:

- How did his parents die?
- How long was he at the Home?
- What were the other orphans like?
- What was the building like?
- What was for dinner yesterday?
- How did he escape?

Explore these questions, and any others that seem relevant, through hot seating. Encourage Jimmy Bean to draw on other books and films featuring orphanages (for example, *Oliver Twist, Annie* and *Hetty Feather*).

You could improvise a scene in which Jimmy Bean, having just escaped, goes from house to house, asking to be taken in and meeting with rejection.

Consolidate the work by getting something down on paper:

- Draw a picture of the orphanage – the building; the Matron; a dormitory.
- Draw a picture of Jimmy Bean by the side of the road.
- Write a diary of what has happened today.
- Write a letter to a local resident asking to be taken in.
- Write a five-point wish list.

Despite the differences between them, Pollyanna and Jimmy Bean have something significant in common: she is also an orphan. Ask your actors to agree together a list of the difficulties that come from being orphaned. What is Pollyanna's reaction when Jimmy Bean first mentions the Orphans' Home?

Cheering Up

Pollyanna's charm is irresistible. Though Jimmy Bean holds out at first, he soon gives way. By the end of the scene, his mood has brightened. A sad-to-happy improvisation will give Pollyanna a chance to practise cheering Jimmy Bean up and Jimmy Bean a chance to practise his change of mood. Give a location and two characters; one cheerful, the other miserable. During a one-minute scene, the miserable character's mood transforms until he is laughing.

Listening

Jimmy Bean has one speech, and Pollyanna has three. Listening attentively to a long speech you have heard many times before is a challenge for any actor. Characters rarely set out to 'make speeches'; sometimes the ideas and the words just flow. The listener must follow as though hearing these ideas for the first time. During a speech, pause the scene and then unfreeze the listener. What is he or she thinking? (This is known as thought tracking.)

Concentration is essential to listening. Tune your actors into each other with some concentration games. See the box on Circle Time on page 65.

Pace and Pause

Jimmy Bean's final line gives a strong clue that Pollyanna talks nineteen to the dozen. Yet if everything comes out in a torrent, some light and shade will be lacking. Help your actors to vary their pace and find appropriate pauses to give the whole scene variety.

The pace of a scene depends less on quick talking than it does on quick reactions. How does the scene run if Pollyanna is very quick on her cues, whereas Jimmy Bean mulls before he speaks? How about the reverse? Ask Jimmy Bean to speak slowly. What is the effect?

Ask Pollyanna to try putting pauses in her third and fourth lines. During the pause she might scrutinise Jimmy Bean or look at the landscape. What did she find herself thinking about during the pauses? Did they feel right? If not, take them back out and look elsewhere.

BEST FRIENDS
adapted by David Lawson Lean from Jacqueline Wilson ✳ *Acting Anthology page 90*

Knowing Each Other Inside Out

The source for this story, a novel by Jacqueline Wilson published in 2004, will almost certainly appeal to your actors, especially if they have chosen this scene themselves. If they haven't read the book already (and unless they struggle with reading), they shouldn't need much encouragement. Reading it will give them useful background on the nature and history of the friendship between **Gemma** and **Alice** and will provide a context and location for the scene.

Project Work
- CHARACTER WORKSHEET
- KNOWLEDGE NOTES
- STAGE DIAGRAM
- ART: *Other character*
- WRITING: *Shared experiences*

GLOSSARY

disagreement	burble	firm
feebly	nosy	brought up short
stricken	settled	longed
sneaky	wailing	bitterly
peeps		
get on everyone's nerves		

The extremely close friendship between the two girls underpins the drama, and you should help your actors to immerse themselves in the circumstances of their relationship. Whether they take details from the novel, invent their own back story or embellish the source with their own ideas, ask your actors to work together to chart Gemma and Alice's life until now. Depending on your students, give them a writing, drawing or improvisation task (or all three) along the following lines:

- The girls list (then describe to you) their ten most important shared experiences.
- The girls devise a short scene telling the story of their lives so far.
- Each girl draws the other's character and annotates her picture with her friend's many positive attributes.

BFF

The girls have a close friendship and are comfortable with physical contact with each other; early in the scene, Gemma touches Alice's lips. Your actors might or might not leap straight into this. You could play a few group or pair games that involve physical contact in order to relax them into the intimacy they need for the scene:

- ELBOW TO ELBOW!
  Students mill around the room; you call out two body parts ('knee to knee!'; 'shoulder to shoulder!'), and they immediately find a partner and make contact accordingly. If the body parts are different, the contact must be doubled – 'ear to hand!' means each student has an ear on the other's hand. In a group, the slowest pair goes out (see page 13).
- TWISTER
  Set up a version of this classic game (great for stretching and body control) using pieces of coloured paper or mats on the floor. Draw cards from a hat to decide which hand/foot must be placed on which colour.

- CONSULT THE ORACLE

  Find a big coat or other garment that both actors can fit into and button it up so that they become a single being with two heads. Place this being (The Oracle) in a temple. Now you (or classmates), after paying appropariate homage, consult The Oracle for advice on a future course of action. The Oracle replies, each head speaking one word in turn.

- TRUST ME

  Pair up the students. One is blindfolded, the other must hop. They have to move across the room without crashing. (Ideas for other trust exercises, great for fostering good relationships among students, can be downloaded from the web page which accompanies this book.)

What's on Your Mind?

At the start of the scene, Gemma and Alice are both keeping a secret (unusual for girls who have always shared everything). Investigate their private feelings and explore why they are keeping them private (because the truth frightens them) in order to build the tense atmosphere which is essential to the drama.

Work through the scene slowly. At frequent intervals you give a signal, and the actors freeze. Tap one to unfreeze her. Explain that she can talk freely, since the other character is still frozen and won't hear anything she says. Ask her to explain what's on her mind.

Your first freeze might come at the very beginning. If you unfreeze Alice, she might confess that she needs to tell Gemma about the house move but doesn't know how. If you unfreeze Gemma, she might confess her fear that Alice doesn't want to be her best friend any more.

Work through the scene, exploring the turmoil in the girls' minds as each struggles with the terrible idea that their friendship might be over. Examine the effect that each piece of new information has on the girls' moods and thoughts.

When you run the scene again, allow them to go as slowly as they want. Give them time to absorb the layers of emotion underneath their words.

Opposites Attract

For all their closeness (they even share Gemma's dog, Barking Mad), Gemma and Alice are very different from each other. In some respects, they are polar opposites. Ask your actors to list all their differences in two columns: talker/listener; active/contemplative; footballer/artist and so on. Again, they can take their details from Jacqueline Wilson or imagine their own.

Once you have explored their differences, you could run a version of the classic TV quiz *Mr & Mrs*. Give each girl five or ten questions. Base them on past experiences, preferences, and hypothetical 'What would you do if?'s. They write their answers privately. Then stage a quiz show in which each must guess what the other answered. Discuss the answers so that they deepen their understanding of each other and themselves.

Finally, ask your students to think about how to find contrast in their performances – in what ways might Gemma and Alice sit, stand, move and speak differently from each other?

The Prop

Marshall and **Leigh** spend most of this scene rigging up a fake ghost to scare their big cousin Errol. They construct their ghost from a pole and bedsheets and embellish it by putting a hat on it and sprinkling flour, rum and black pepper around it. Real flour, rum and pepper would make a mess. You could mime them altogether or use an empty flour bag, rum bottle and pepperpot.

Is it a good idea to use a real pole and sheets? On the one hand, the contraption is central to the scene; the boys are busy with it throughout. On the other hand, it could be distracting and awkward for your youngsters.

The pole needs to stand up. A garden umbrella stand would work in the right way, as long as the boys could easily set it and strike it. A plastic stand designed to be filled with water (but empty) might be manageable. The umbrella itself would give some spread for the ghost's arms. Alternatively, you could tape two old broomsticks together to make a cross.

If you decide that you want a real prop, bring in some materials and challenge your actors to make something themselves. (Observe them as they do so – their interactions might give you some useful ideas when it comes to directing the scene.) Turn the lights off – have they made something that looks genuinely scary in the dark?

It would be perfectly acceptable to mime the prop, but your actors will have to work hard to convince their audience that it is there. Ask them together to draw pictures of Marshall and Leigh's scarecrow ghost so that everyone is agreed on what it looks like.

More reflections on using props in LAMDA exams are on page 41.

Project Work

- CHARACTER WORKSHEET
- KNOWLEDGE NOTES
- STAGE DIAGRAM
- RESEARCH: Village in, eg, Jamaica
- OBSERVATION: The world at night
- OUTING: Night-time walk
- ART: The scarecrow ghost

GLOSSARY

workmate	intruder	special effects
rum	dissolve	sprinkle
cautiously	cemetery	uncontrollably
bundle	vanish	crouch
full of himself	midwife	approach
prance	shudder	

Keeping It Down

If your actors have not visited a Caribbean village, this location might seem exotic. Yet the key features of the setting are its quietness and its darkness. Ask them to think of an alleyway or village path they have been in and to describe it in detail. From this basis they can add a few local details with an online image search (the word *Caribbean* returns lots of photos of holiday resorts, so pick a specific country).

Marshall and Leigh must speak quietly so that they are not caught. Yet your actors need to perform with energy and project their voices. They'll need to master a stage whisper (if they really whisper, they won't be heard and may hurt their throats):

- They speak at a slightly lower volume than usual but exaggerate their mouth movements. Doing so will give the impression that they are striving to be heard by their scene partner but not overheard. In terms of projection, what they sacrifice in volume they should gain in clarity.
- They 'sell' the stage whisper by looking around to check that nobody can hear them and signalling to each other to keep the volume down.
- The effort to be quiet also applies to any physical acting: they creep rather than walk and handle noisy items carefully.

Working at Night

It is late at night. Even if there is electric light in this village, there won't be much illumination, and the boys might be working by the light of the moon.

You can establish the night time setting right at the outset. The boys enter from different directions and don't see each other at first; Marshall sees Leigh and calls to him; then Leigh (perhaps after a moment) spots Marshall.

How is the world different at night, and how does that affect a person's mood and behaviour? Ask your students to observe the world and themselves next time they find themselves outdoors at night. What can they hear that they wouldn't hear during the day? Do they speak and act differently?

In later rehearsals, when you have the scene up and running, play it with the lights dimmed or even off.

Teaming Up

There are subtle but important differences in personality between Marshall and Leigh. Tease out these differences first by asking questions:

- Whose idea was it to set up a ghost?
- Who brought what with them?
- Where did each of you get all these items?
- Why couldn't each of you manage this without the other's help?

SLIDING SCALE

Follow up your discussion with this exercise. You're still asking questions, but because the exercise invites physical rather than verbal responses, the actors can work more instinctively.

Stand your students centre stage. Far stage left represents '0%, definitely not, never' and far stage right represents '100%, absolutely, always.' You ask questions, and students move to an appropriate position on the scale. These questions are a matter of opinion, not fact: there are no definitive answers, and they may change their minds later on.

If the first question is 'How much fun are you having creating this ghost?', Leigh might be closer to 100% than Marshall, who is more concerned with the dangers and the practicalities. Other questions could include:

- Are you angry when Errol wakes you up with all his noise?
- Do you think this ghost actually looks scary?
- Are you frightened of getting caught?
- Are you excited about Errol's reaction?

Who's In Charge?

Customer is in charge of this situation until the role reversal. As soon as **Waiter** sits down and plays the role of a customer, he takes control, and the real Customer is unable to get it back.

The scene involves a classic status switch. Whether or not you use the word *status,* your students will recognise the idea that in most interactions, someone is more 'in charge'. To perform this scene well, your actors must express status, especially through body language.

Project Work

- CHARACTER WORKSHEET
- KNOWLEDGE NOTES
- STAGE DIAGRAM
- OBSERVATION: *Waiters and customers*
- OUTING: *Restaurant visit*
- ART: *Restaurant menu*

GLOSSARY

impatient	speciality	got the hang of it
water chestnut	veal	demonstrate

Expressing Status

Ask your students to imagine a group of children on a beach building a sandcastle together. There is a lot to figure out – how big it should be, how to make a moat, whose turn it is with the bucket, and so on. Just from watching, how would your students know who was in charge?

The child in charge might be the one giving instructions, expressing authority through the voice. How does she make herself heard above the arguments and the chatter? Why do the other children listen and obey?

The child in charge might be physically dominant, expressing authority through the body. How does she stand? How does she walk around? Where does she look? Why do the other children submit instead of fighting back?

IMPROVISATION

Ask your students to improvise the sandcastle scene. Choose one to be the child in charge; she must get the sandcastle built exactly as she wants it.

* STATUS (1) *

Status is a crucial element of drama. The status of a character is a measure of how much power – or authority, or control – that character has in the current situation. Your students will recognise the concept from their own relationships – with siblings, in the playground and with adults both familiar and unfamiliar.

Status is expressed physically through the whole body. A high-status character occupies her space confidently and comfortably. Her body language is expansive and relaxed. She often makes direct eye contact. A low-status character does her best to avoid being noticed. She fears disapproval or punishment. She doesn't oppose or antagonise. She avoids eye contact and takes up as little space and makes as little noise as possible. Her body language is closed-off and tense.

Status is also expressed in the voice (in the manner of speaking as well as the words spoken). A high-status character speaks fluently and clearly, preventing interruption. A character with low status speaks haltingly (inviting interruption).

What happens if her scene partner or classmates try resisting? How can the child in charge get her way? Encourage your actors not to compete: to tell the story, they must collaborate even when their characters are clashing.

Status Levels

Ask your students to imagine that there is a scale of 'in-chargeness.' It runs from 1 to 10. At number 10, you're totally in control; at 1, you have no control. Play the opening of the scene, stop and ask your students to give each character a number. Customer is in charge. How authoritative is he? Waiter is doing what he is told. How submissive is he?

Continue working through the scene, stopping often to number each character's status. How does a character physically lower down (because he is seated) assert status over someone standing above him? What sort of eye contact will there be between the two? How will they use their voices?

The status switch should be highly entertaining as Waiter takes full control and Customer cannot prevent the rapid downward slide in his status.

Balloon

Finally, for a bit of clownish fun, play the scene, but this time give Customer a balloon. Every time Waiter says or does something silly, Customer can hit Waiter with the balloon. But when he hands over the role of customer, he hands over the balloon with it. The Waiter will enjoy getting his revenge.

Research

What kind of a restaurant is this? If it's an exclusive establishment, both Waiter and Customer might be rather haughty. If it's a beachfront café, they are unlikely to be. Ask your actors to make notes next time they go to a restaurant. Does it seem to be a high-class place? How much does a side order of chips cost? How do waiters (or servers) interact with customers? How is their body language and eye contact? Do the customers always have the higher status?

Further Ideas

- As the scene is short and doesn't involve much movement or business, the dialogue must be really snappy and full of energy. Drill the lines well. Do a run of the scene in which each character repeats the last word or couple of words of the other character's line before speaking his own line.
- When working on status, experiment with energy levels. Although high-status characters often radiate powerful energy, it is possible to express very high status calmly, slowly and quietly. The queen does not shout. A low-status character, on the other hand, might be scrabbling for all he is worth to escape the terrifying situation.
- Explore different ways of playing the opening of the scene and different choices for the underlying characters of Customer and Waiter:
  - Have things already started to go wrong or has it all been fine until now?
  - Does Customer prefer to remain polite and friendly or to show his displeasure? Is he usually patient or irritable?
  - Is Waiter nervous in this job or is he confident? Is he enjoying himself?

THE DARING GAME
adapted by LAMDA from Kit Pearson ✳ *Acting Anthology page 100*

Source and Setting

This scene has been adapted from a Canadian children's novel published in 1987. This conversation is described in Chapter 13, 'Helen Confesses.'

If your students are keen readers, encourage them to get hold of the book. Background reading is a good habit for young actors to form. Immersing themselves in the world **Helen** and **Eliza** inhabit will help them to make valuable contributions during rehearsals and during the Knowledge section of their LAMDA exam. They will learn about the feast, the lost Pound Money, Helen's history and other background. Nevertheless, the scene contains all the essential information, so background reading is optional.

The book is set in Canada, so the assumption is that that's where you'll be setting it. However, if you really want to do this scene with two actors who cannot do a passable Canadian accent, it might be possible to justify using their home accents and setting it in a British boarding school. The Canadian writer's English is much closer to British English than some of the US English scenes in the anthology. Perhaps with this in mind, the adapters have changed the original's only distinctly non-British word, 'lousy', to 'ghastly'.

If you set the scene in Britain, make sure that your actors know why you have made this decision, so that they can discuss it in their LAMDA exam.

Project Work

- CHARACTER WORKSHEET
- KNOWLEDGE NOTES
- STAGE DIAGRAM
- RESEARCH: Boarding school
- ART: Picture for the other character; photo story
- WRITING: Acrostic poem; memory of something you did together

GLOSSARY

boarding school	confront	tag along
responsible	trail off	stingy
challenge authority		ghastly

My Friend

Can your actors identify what each character wants from this exchange? One answer might be that Eliza wants Helen to tell the truth, and Helen wants Eliza to understand and believe her. For the scene to have drama, the wants – whatever you decide they are – must be powerful. In other words, the stakes are high; the consequences of either character not getting what she wants are very bad. The scene should have a journey, so that by the end, all the truth-telling has changed something important about the girls' friendship.

To uncover the scene's deeper truths, help your actors to burrow into the relationship between Helen and Eliza. Hot-seat each girl, but ask her questions about the other character. You could be in role as the school's welfare officer or a form tutor. Here are some questions you could ask Helen:

- What do you like about Eliza?
- What is Eliza's worst characteristic?
- Is there anything about Eliza that worries or scares you?
- Has the friendship with Eliza changed you?
- Do you have any secrets from Eliza?

As the girls continue to think about their friendship in general terms, consolidate by getting some ideas onto paper:

- Draw a picture that you think Eliza will like.
- Write an acrostic poem about Eliza.
- Rummage through the props cupboard and find something that relates to something you and Eliza did together. Draw the object and write a paragraph describing the event.

Emotional Tableaux

Even before they start speaking, the girls are at odds. Investigate with your actors what is on each character's mind at the opening, then ask them to translate that dynamic into a frozen picture or tableau.

Begin the dialogue, and stop again when you or the actors feel a major shift. You should all feel a big change when Helen realises that Eliza is not listening. Again, spend some time investigating what is going on here. Why is Eliza so hesitant about asking Helen the question? How does Helen feel when she realises Eliza is not listening? When Eliza does ask her the question, why is her answer so direct?

Again, ask the girls to make a stage picture. Encourage them to be bold in their body shape, positioning and facial expression. Continue through the scene, creating tableaux for each turning point.

Follow-Up: Photo Story

Take a photo of each tableau the girls create. Arrange the photos into sequence on a side or two of A4. Leave space around each one. Give a printout to each of the girls and ask them to add speech bubbles or thought bubbles to create a photo story of the scene.

Situation: Verbal Sumo

Another way of looking at the scene's shifting dynamic would be to set it up as a (contactless) sumo wrestling match. Mark out a circle on the floor. Stand both actors in the centre. Explain that whenever an actor feels that her character is strong, she should take forward steps. Whenever she feels that her character is weak, she should take backward steps.

They move together: when one moves forwards, the other moves backwards.

Your actors might grasp the exercise without any need for clarification. If they are unsure, show that a character is 'strong' when she is directing lots of energy towards the other character. This might be when she is accusing, entertaining, interrogating or informing. A character is 'weak' when she is directing negative energy at herself or just receiving the other character's positive energy. This might be when she is apologising, confessing, pleading, or listening.

Let your actors play through the scene to discover its ebb and flow. Insist on eye contact. Look for moments where you might play against the obvious: an apology might be agressive, or an accusation might be a flustered retreat.

Situation: Beat to Beat

After reading through this scene for the first time, ask your actors to retell the main story points in a bulletpointed list (around ten should be right). Each bulletpoint describes an important moment in the scene (sometimes called a beat). Help them to get started. The first one should be quite obvious. The complete list might run as follows:

- **Andy** and **Corry** squeeze into the train.
- They recall going through the station.
- They absorb their surroundings.
- Corry reveals he's never been on one of these trains.
- Andy reveals he's never been on one of these trains.
- Corry realises they're going the wrong way.
- Andy realises they're going the wrong way.
- They try to figure out what to do.
- They realise the train is empty.
- They jump out.

> ### Project Work
> - CHARACTER WORKSHEET
> - KNOWLEDGE NOTES
> - STAGE DIAGRAM
> - RESEARCH: Underground train carriage
> - OBSERVATION: Jiggling around
> - OUTING: Underground train trip
> - ART: Andy and Corry on the train
> GLOSSARY
>
> | | | |
> |---|---|---|
> | escalator | rush hour | strain |
> | luggage | rely on | strap hang |

When your students have come up with their list, check it through and then use it as a basis for your initial work.

- Test their understanding of the journey through the scene by chopping up the list and asking them to put the events in order.
- Project the list onto the wall where the actors will see it (alternatively, use a flipchart or large pieces of paper held up by classmates). Play through the scene, revealing each new beat as the actors reach it.
- Ask your actors to devise a tableau for each bulletpoint (encourage strong facial expression).
  - Take a photo of each tableau, print the photos and ask your actors to sequence them.
  - Print the whole sequence and ask your actors to add speech and thought bubbles to make a photo story.
  - As you read each bulletpoint, your actors form the tableau. Can they perform the entire sequence from memory, like a human slideshow?

Location

Get to know precise details of the location of this scene. There is not much scope for your actors to move in their crowded and confined environment. A rich knowledge of their surroundings might produce some business which will prevent the scene from becoming too static. It will also give them plenty to talk about when their LAMDA examiner asks them where the scene is set.

✳ CHARACTER WORKSHEETS ✳

*C*haracter worksheets are an essential part of your teaching toolkit. For a young actor, drawing a picture of his character and writing down some biographical information (age, family, likes and dislikes) instills the idea that he is creating someone or something distinct from himself. The character is something the actor steps into and out of. All the while he is in character, he will have to speak differently, think differently, and react differently from the way he speaks, thinks and reacts in real life. Most youngsters will grasp this concept but might struggle to sustain a performance. The more of his own ideas your actor has applied in creating the character, the more likely he is to be able to step in and stay in.

For older actors, creating and understanding a back story focuses attention on what lies behind a character's decisions and actions. They begin to understand how what a person feels, says and thinks springs from life-experience and from underlying character traits.

A character might exist vividly in your actor's imagination. Encourage him to carry his character around with him and to imagine how his character would react in situations the actor finds himself in. Give him art and writing tasks to embellish the basic biography. He might cut pictures out of magazines to stick in a scrap book, write diary entries or make a playlist.

Character worksheets can be downloaded from the web page which accompanies this book.

There are various ways of stimulating ideas about the setting:
- Start with the text: examine the boys' observations of their surroundings.
- If you live in a city with an underground train system, arrange a research trip – ideally at a busy time. The actors should make notes and take photos.
- If your actors have ever been on an underground train, what can they remember about the experience?
- Look at online photos and videos of underground train carriages.

When your actors have plenty of ideas, ask them to draw their characters on the train. Also, hot-seat them in situ. They start playing the scene; you freeze them and ask them very detailed questions about what is around them. Encourage them to think freely and spontaneously. Questions might include:
- Who is sitting exactly opposite you?
- What is the main story on the page of the man's newspaper?
- What colour are the seats?
- What's the loudest noise?

Playing the Setting

With little scope for movement, your actors will need to evoke the setting through quite subtle use of their voices and bodies. How loudly can they speak without being heard by their fellow passengers? Is the train very shaky, jiggling them around in their seats? Is there any activity among their fellow passengers which takes their attention?

Character

Your actors are free to decide what age, gender and personality type Andy and Corry are. They can and should create full back stories for their characters and also agree on the relationship between them. Start the work by filling in a character worksheet (see box, above).

Finding Differences

The differences between **Eliza** and **Jane** might not be immediately obvious to your actors, but it is important for the drama that they find and play the points of contrast. Help them to tease out the differences by analysing the text.

Take the moment where Jane wriggles her toes in a rock pool. What is Eliza's reaction? Together, come up with three words (or phrases) that might pop into each character's head when they see the rock pool. Jane might have 'play, wriggle, cool', whereas Eliza might have 'silly, waste of time, fossils.'

Ask your actors to look at other moments in the scene where the girls have different reactions to the same object or circumstance. Ask them to come up with three words each for:

- The pile of rocks (when they first see it)
- The first brown stone
- The Back Lane boys arriving
- The Back Lane boys running away
- The big fossil (at the end of the scene)

The actors take the stage. Call out an item from the list; they speak their three words, one at a time in turn. Ask them to speak their words at each other as though they are disagreeing. Repeat the exercise, asking them to strike a full-body pose – whatever comes to mind – as they speak each word. The word should be expressed spontaneously through the whole body.

Finally, come together to discuss what character traits have started to emerge. Eliza's words will have been more authoritative and serious, Jane's more playful and questioning. Were there any threads or patterns in the body shapes that might help with physicality for the characters?

FOLLOW-UP: SPIDER DIAGRAM

Each girl can draw a spider diagram with all her words emanating from a drawing of her character. Any traits they have settled on in your discussion can be added to this sheet, as can the events you pinned this exercise around.

The Back Lane Boys

Let your actors decide how many Back Lane boys there are, and choose classmates (if you have them) to stand in. Improvise a couple of lines for them.

If the boys approach from the audience (ie, the back of your classroom or rehearsal space), the girls will be able to play the distance effectively, and their attention will be directed out front.

Project Work

- CHARACTER WORKSHEET
- KNOWLEDGE NOTES
- STAGE DIAGRAM
- RESEARCH: Fossils; beach
- OBSERVATION: Sand and water
- OUTING: Beach trip
- ART: Spider diagram; setting

GLOSSARY

fossil	undercut	promising
Victorian	goodly	the like of
craze	reluctant	fed up
significant	discard	wheelbarrow
specimen	shard	

Both the girls are down – Jane sitting and Eliza kneeling. When you rehearse with stand-ins, the girls should get used to where they must look in order to make eye contact with Scrummer and his gang.

Encourage committed characterisation from the boys and plenty of interplay. The first time you take the stand-ins away, can the girls perform exactly as they did when they had real Back Lane boys to play off?

The Setting

Ask your actors to comb through the text and make a list of every bit of information it offers about the location. If you live near the coast, your girls should try to arrange a seaside trip together. Can they find a rock pool, a brown stone, a rock face and other items in their list? How does it feel to walk barefoot on sand? How does it feel to step from sand into water and back out again? If they have visited a beach recently, ask them for recollections. (See page 110 for more ideas on a beach trip.) Alternatively, they can look in magazines or search online for useful beach photos. Use all the information gathered to draw a picture or make a collage of the setting. When you have a clear picture, map out the stage. Where is the sea? Where is the path leading up to the village?

❋ NO PEEKING! ❋

Taking a quick peek at the teacher or examiner during an acted scene is a common habit that some young actors find hard to shake off. They want to check that they are being watched attentively and approvingly. Yet they are supposed to be immersed in an imaginary world. Eye contact between them and you (or the examiner) shatters the illusion.

Reassuring them that lots of actors do it, tell habitual peekers that it's important to learn not to. Promise them that when they are acting you are watching them from beginning to end. Tell them that you have been specially trained to write notes and watch the stage at the same time. Their examiner will be writing notes during their performance but will be watching the whole time.

From Entry Level to Grade 5, the Assessment Criteria stipulate the need to 'perform... with fluency and focus'. Do plenty of concentration and focus exercises with habitual peekers. During rehearsal, whenever you catch a peek, ask your actor what her character is doing and thinking – and if she can't come up with an answer, suggest one to take her focus back into the scene.

Costume
The girls are barefoot. If both have trousers rolled up to the knees (or skirts hitched up) and shoes around their necks, they'll do much to establish the location before they even speak.

Further Ideas
- Why is it so important to the girls to find fossils? Find a back-story that involves high stakes: what are the consequences for the girls if they come home empty-handed?
- Will real props serve this scene well? Can your girls easily manage baskets and tools in their exam (see page 41)? What will you use for the big rock that Jane sits on?

INTERPRETATION – 20 marks for each scene (40 total)
L01 Perform two scenes from memory, demonstrating an understanding of the material.

Does your student...	**Pass**	**Merit**	**Distinction**
Understand the MEANING of the words she is speaking?	Some	Most	All
Communicate the meaning of the words?	Some	Most	All
Understand the CHARACTER and the SITUATION?	Some of the time	Most of the time	All of the time
Communicate the character and the situation?	Some of the time	Most of the time	All of the time
Know the LINES?	Quite well	Well	Perfectly
Stay IMMERSED in the imaginary world?	Some of the time	Most of the time	Throughout

TECHNIQUE – 20 marks for each scene (40 total)
L02 Use vocal skills in response to the text. ❋ L03 Use the performance space in response to the text.

Does your student...	**Pass**	**Merit**	**Distinction**
PROJECT (speak clearly and with appropriate volume)?	Some of the time	Most of the time	All of the time
PAUSE for thought or to let unseen characters speak?	Some of the time	Most of the time	All of the time
Vary PACE to express different emotions?	Some of the time	Most of the time	All of the time
Use appropriate MOVEMENT in the performance?	Some of the time	Most of the time	All of the time

KNOWLEDGE – 20 marks overall (conversation with the examiner)
L04 Know and understand the characters and situations in the chosen scenes.

Can your student discuss...	**Pass**	**Merit**	**Distinction**
The LOCATION of both scenes?	Briefly	Securely	In detail
What both characters ARE DOING during the scenes?	Briefly	Securely	In detail
The FEELINGS of both characters during the scenes?	Briefly	Securely	In detail
The MOOD of both scenes?	Briefly	Securely	In detail

Distinction: 80–100 • Merit 65–79 • Pass: 50–64

A learner fails if

- She scores 49 marks or less overall OR
- She scores 0 in one or more of the assessment criteria (L01, L02 etc)

FORMAT: SOLO EXAMS (15 MINUTES ALLOWED) AND DUOLOGUE EXAMS (20 MINUTES)

- 1 set scene from the *LAMDA Acting Anthology, Volume 3*
- 1 own-choice scene (between 2 and 3 minutes)
- Conversation

FORMAT: COMBINED EXAMS (25 MINUTES ALLOWED)

- 1 set duologue from the *LAMDA Acting Anthology, Volume 3*
- 2 own-choice solo scenes (between 2 and 3 minutes each)
- Conversation… OR
- 2 set solo scenes from the *LAMDA Acting Anthology, Volume 3*
- 1 own-choice duologue (between 2 and 3 minutes)
- Conversation

Scenes may be performed in any order.

Learners must announce the title, author and character of each scene before performing it. Decide on the phrasing and practise plenty of times:

- *For my set scene, I will be performing… by… I am playing the part of…*
- *My own-choice scene is… by… and I will be playing…*

Consider including a brief (one- or two-sentence) explanation of the context if your actors can manage it. It shows they have thought about their scene and adds polish to their performance. If an own-choice scene is not familiar to the examiner, the context will be useful.

Get students to test each other. Recruit family to help at home. Explore **line-learning** techniques. Work on picking up **cues**.

Go through the glossary.

Walk around the room, varying speed according to the character's emotional energy (see page 25). Look for high-tempo feelings (excitement, panic) and low-tempo feelings (sadness, exhaustion).

Insist on no peeking (see page 87).

Use **circle time** for conversation practice.

Complete a stage diagram. Do a guided tour (see page 57). Make a picture of the setting.

During runs, sit at the back of the room or close your eyes: can you hear the words? Do **voice** exercises and **tongue-twisters**.

CHECKLIST: GRADE 3

Do you…
- ☐ know your lines?
- ☐ understand all of the words?
- ☐ project (a strong clear voice)?
- ☐ use pauses?
- ☐ vary the pace?
- ☐ move during the scene?
- ☐ stay in character?

Can you describe…
- ☐ your character's feelings?
- ☐ the location of the scene?
- ☐ your character's actions?
- ☐ the mood of the scene?

Look at the character's **wants**. Divide the scene into **chapters**. You read words; student performs the **actions**.

Look at **transitions** from one feeling or idea to the next. Make sure each thought occupies its own space (see page 24).

Work on physical characterisation. Do some **tableau** exercises.

Do **thought tracking**. Do abstract drawings or colour the script using **colours for feelings**. Do plenty of **hot seating**.

On a spider diagram, list:
- Feelings experienced in the scene
- Location or locations of the scene
- Pace of the scene
- Key words and images
- Anything unusual

What adjective or adjectives belong at the centre of the diagram?

---

*Words in **bold text** can be found in the index.*

Source

The source for this scene is the second chapter – 'In which Sophie is compelled to seek her fortune' – of a children's novel published in 1986. The adaptation is relatively loose, and reading the relevant chapter might enrich your student's understanding of the character and situation and inspire her to read the whole book.

Unseen Character

Pick a classmate to stand in for the unseen Wicked Witch of the Waste. She and **Sophie** can script lines and actions for the witch and then rehearse that part of the scene. Sophie's reactions to the witch, together with the stage directions, give plenty of clues.

Encourage strong characterisation and a committed performance from the stand-in, so that the witch remains imprinted on the scene when you take her out. Pay particular attention to the moment when the witch reveals her face. Sophie's reaction is an immediate switch from annoyance to terror, expressed through the whole body (she jumps back).

GAME: HOW FRIGHTENED AM I?

Stretch your students' acting muscles and extend the range of their expressiveness with a guessing game. Remove the court cards from a deck so that you have four jumbled sets of cards numbered from 1 to 10. Students in turn pick a card and express fear on a scale from 1 (mildly worried) to 10 (utterly petrified). Use the line from the scene – 'Oh my goodness', accompanied by a backwards jump. To make the reaction a sudden one, shout 'Witch!' as a cue.

Other students guess the number and declare their guess by holding up a card from their own set (or by writing the number on a piece of paper). Set up a competition by awarding a point to each correct guesser. The performer gets a point for every correct guess (since the real skill is in the acting).

Finish up by deciding with Sophie what number she will play the reaction at in her performance.

Sophie's Focus

Your actor has to negotiate several switches of focus. You and she can use points of focus as stepping stones when mapping out the scene.

As the scene opens, Sophie is addressing the cherry hat. When does her focus switch and to what? (It's when she picks up the the black and white hat). Next she addresses all the hats together. Where does her focus then go? She recalls the complaining customer from earlier in the day, and although

Project Work

- CHARACTER WORKSHEET
- KNOWLEDGE NOTES
- STAGE DIAGRAM
- OBSERVATION: *Old people*
- ART: *Wicked Witch of the Waste*
- WRITING: *Hat characters*

GLOSSARY

late	storm	flinch
whirl	sable	hobble
pleated	wrap	
bonnet	plume	

she is ostensibly talking to the hats, the vivid memory absorbs her. Your actor might switch her focus to the remembered customer and return to the hats as she finishes the recollection.

When the grand-looking customer enters, Sophie can choose where to address her commentary and her sardonic remark – to one of the previous hats, or a new one. During their conversation, Sophie is focused on the customer. After the powder is sprinkled, Sophie's focus remains on the witch until she leaves the shop; then she focuses on herself and finally on her reflection in the mirror.

✻ VOICE WARM-UP ✻

*V*oice work should form part of any drama class. There are plenty of ways of making voice exercises playful for younger actors. Most will enjoy inflating themselves like balloons (and then spinning around the room making raspberry noises); pulling crazy animal faces; catching flies with their tongue; drawing pitch rollercoasters in the air; buzzing like bees and miaowing like cats; and of course practising tongue-twisters, especially the slightly rude ones. Every time a student laughs a proper belly laugh, congratulate her on using her diaphragm. See page 21 for some thoughts on using tongue-twisters in your drama class.

Sophie and Her Hats

Sophie talks to her hats as though they were alive. Explore this relationship – your actor can play the opening sections of the scene as though she were a schoolmistress talking to young children; a cat enthusiast with her pets; a teenager gossiping with friends, or any other scenarios that spring to mind.

She might characterise her hats: a cheeky one, a shy one, a bossy one and so on. A hat on a higher stand might have higher status than one on a low shelf. A stage diagram will help to fix the layout of her shop. Can she address and handle the different hats in subtly different ways?

The Ageing Spell

The climax of the scene is Sophie's dramatic transformation into an Old Woman. Playing this transformation will give a whole class enjoyable practice at body control and physical characterisation.

- Your students space out in the room and adopt a relaxed but energised pose. As you call out parts of the body, they clench and then relax. Include toes, knees, buttocks, hands, shoulders and parts of the face.
- Now they imagine they are very old indeed. They choose parts of their body which are stiff or painful, and over a count of ten, they stiffen up.
- When they are fully aged, ask them in turn to say something – a tongue-twister, today's date, the first line of a poem. Encourage croaks, wheezes and whistles but insist on clarity. Then count down from five to one to release them back to youth.
- Repeat the ageing process with students walking around the room, dancing, or playing hopscotch.
- If you have time, ask your elderly characters to tell you something about themselves and their views on life. Keep it free and fun. You could have a game of Old Person It. Students are out if they move too youthfully.

Source Text

This meeting between Beauty and **Ginger** occurs in Chapter 40 ('Poor Ginger') of Anna Sewell's classic novel, published in 1877. Encourage your students to read this chapter (but be warned – it ends badly for Ginger).

Black Beauty deserves a place on every child's bookshelf. It hooks many young readers and stays with them for life. Reading the whole book is by no means essential, but it will benefit your actor's performance, increase her sense of ownership of the scene and fuel some interesting discussion in the Knowledge section of her exam.

Project Work

- CHARACTER WORKSHEET
- KNOWLEDGE NOTES
- STAGE DIAGRAM
- RESEARCH: *Horse paintings/videos*
- OBSERVATION: *Horses*
- ART: *Open countryside/Earlshall*
- WRITING: *Spider diagram: youth*
- GLOSSARY

mare	*canter*	*ill-used*
shabby	*gallop*	*bear*
cab	*suppress*	*knackers*
sidle	*strain*	*newfound*
wistful	*bout*	

Context

There are references in this scene to past events and circumstances that it is useful to know. The horses were both injured while together at Earlshall; Beauty when ridden clumsily by a drunk Reuben Smith, and Ginger when ridden too hard by the reckless Lord George. Black Beauty was sold off straight away, and Ginger was given a year in the meadow before being sold.

The scene takes place at a cab rank outside a London park.

Equine Physicality

The balance between horse and human needs to be delicately struck. Ginger's words and emotions are sophisticated, human ones. Yet the experiences that have produced those emotions – especially her mistreatment by people – belong to a horse, as do her memories of happier days.

You could begin working on the physical characterisation by looking at paintings of horses. The most skillful horse painters give their subjects remarkable expressiveness. Look at paintings by George Stubbs, James Ward, John Frederick Herring Sr and Alfred Munnings for inspiration. You'll find plenty of examples of their work online – your student can do some research at home or in a quiet corner of the class.

Can she find horses that put her in mind of Ginger, either now (weary and worn out) or as she used to be (proud and beautiful)?

Gather a selection of horse pictures and challenge your actor to take the stage and choose one of the horses to imitate in a frozen tableau. You and classmates can guess which horse she is portraying.

Which elements of the horse portrait was she most inclined to mimic? Where in her body did she take a different shape? Look together at the eyes, the chest and the line up the back of the neck and over the top of the head.

Your actor won't be able to perform on all fours. You could experiment with using two sticks (held like walking sticks) as spindly front legs.

Equine Movement

A YouTube search for 'horses in motion' returns some useful material from which to draw ideas for Ginger's movements around the stage. Ask your student to look for the most uniquely horsey movements – shifts of weight, tosses of the head, stamps of the foot and so on. As always, make sure that any online research is closely monitored, either by you or by a parent, so that your student does not stumble across something inappropriate. See page 9 for advice on working safely online.

Last Legs

Finally, you need to age poor Ginger. The novel describes the worn-out chestnut's decline from youthful vigour in quite some detail: she has an ill-kept coat, protruding bones, misshapen joints, knuckled knees, unsteady fore-legs, a thin neck, a dull eye, swollen fetlocks (ankle joints), heaving sides, a suffering face and a frequent cough.

Which of these parts of Ginger's body might you incorporate into the performance in order to bring age and neglect into her horse physicality?

Other Character

If possible, involve one or more classmates in the physical work with Ginger, so that you have a stand-in to play Black Beauty. The years have been kinder to him, so he needn't be quite as frail as Ginger.

Black Beauty's main job is to listen actively to Ginger and to react strongly wherever possible. Ginger could script a few short lines or interjections for Beauty if that would help them play off each other and give Ginger an impetus to keep speaking. Beauty is struck by the change in Ginger since he last saw her and very interested in – and moved by – the story she has to tell.

Mood: Nostalgia

This scene is shot through with regret. 'And so… here we are,' Ginger ruefully reflects in Chapter 27, 'ruined in the prime of our youth and strength, you by a drunkard, and I by a fool'.

The wistful, melancholy mood depends on comparing the happiness and freedom of youth with the sad decline of old age. Ginger's memories of the past should be vivid for your actor. She can use Ginger's brief mention of running through 'acres of fresh green countryside' as the basis for imagining life at Earlshall for Ginger.

Put your actor in the hot seat and question her about the past she remembers so fondly. Try to find as many points of contrast with the present. Focus on the body. How well does she remember cantering and galloping, free from aches and pains?

Consolidate this work with a drawing of the open countryside of Ginger's youth or a spider diagram with the word 'youth' at the centre.

Source

The writer of this scene has invented a scenario loosely based on a circumstance in Shakespeare's *The Merchant of Venice*. In the play, Portia leaves Lorenzo and Jessica in charge of her house in Belmont while she heads for Venice. The character of **Mario/Maria** does not appear in the original, and Shakespeare's Jessica is not the immature bossy-boots that Maria describes. Jessica is, however, reported to have exchanged a turquoise ring (stolen from her father, Shylock) for a monkey.

Project Work

- CHARACTER WORKSHEET
- KNOWLEDGE NOTES
- STAGE DIAGRAM
- RESEARCH: *Vegetable preparation*
- ART: *Monkey drawing or puppet*
- WRITING: *Letter of resignation*

GLOSSARY

utensils	tinker	sneer
heiress	hang out	candied
flounce	casket	steward
chamber	courtyard	brandish
mistress	make a bee-line	

The Business

The preamble states that Mario is preparing food at a big table. The stage directions have him pouring a jug of water into a pot at the fireplace and tossing in vegetables before returning to the table to continue chopping.

Having Mario busy with his vegetables throughout will give the scene energy. You could create light and shade by finding moments when he is very focused on the task and moments when his mind is taken up by something else (especially the monkey). The business of chopping vegetables and adding them to the pot will give plenty of opportunities for colour and detail as he expresses emotion through the way he works.

You can approach the challenging business in a number of ways:

- Let the ideas arise spontaneously: ask your actor to do the scene while miming chopping and cooking and see what happens. He'll need both hands free, so use a copy of the script that will sit flat on the table.
- Work on the business off the text: your actor mimes chopping carrots, you read out emotion words, and he expresses that emotion in his chopping. Anger and frustration should be straightforward, but can he chop enviously or despairingly?
- For Mario, this is an everyday task, one he probably does on auto-pilot. Can your actor chop vegetables while concentrating on something else? As he chops, ask him to describe a typical Friday at school, every member of his family or the exact layout of his house.
- Different vegetables need to be prepared in different ways. Cauliflowers need to be stripped, carrots need to be scrubbed, peas need to be shelled and so on. Practise a range of preparations, and call out various vegetables as he works through the scene. Decide where on the table each vegetable is and map it out on a stage diagram.
- As rehearsals progress, find particular words in the scene that might be accompanied by expressive actions – 'flounces' might be a good

word on which to throw vegetables into the pot, and 'tinkers' might be accompanied by a firm chop.

Character: At the End of His Tether

Mario is very worked up – with your actor, make a list of everything that is causing his blood to boil and investigate why.

- THE MONKEY

  Mario refers to the monkey as a 'nasty little creature', a 'horrible creature', a 'little devil' and a 'little monster'. He would like to jump on it. Why is his hatred for the monkey so strong? With the script to one side, can your actor explain in his own words what the monkey did with the pots and pans, candied fruits and eggs?

  With the facts established, Mario can be more inventive. What does the monkey look like? What noise does it make? He could draw or impersonate the monkey. He could make a monkey puppet from scratch or using a cuddly toy. You could improvise scenes in which the monkey causes havoc in the kitchen and integrate the monkey puppet (with a classmate as operator) into rehearsals of the scene.

- THE TINKER

  The hated monkey came, in Mario's words, from 'one of those tinkers from down south'. The tinker drives a hard bargain, and 'his nasty little tinker eyes light up' when he sees Jessica's ring. Mario clearly hates tinkers. Investigate this opinion with your actor. What is it about tinkers that arouses such contempt in Mario?

- JESSICA

  Mario holds Jessica ultimately responsible for all the monkey's misdeeds. The purchase was ridiculous, and the freedom she allows it is highly irresponsible. What else does he dislike about Jessica? Ask him to do an impersonation of Jessica, using the words he quotes from her. Develop this into an improvisation: recruit a classmate (or join in yourself) and play the scene between Jessica and the tinker. Your actor can play first one part and then the other. Encourage high lampoonery – he can pour all his scorn and contempt into the characterisations.

All this anger, together with clear visualisations of the characters and scenes he is describing, should make for a lively performance.

Further Ideas

- Make a clear decision about Mario's train of thought when he switches from recalling Jessica's arrival to telling the story of the monkey (on 'So what happens?').
- Give Mario further practice at feeling frustration by asking him to read the scene while picking up tennis balls (or whatever you have) from the floor and putting them in a bucket. Limit the number he can carry at a time. When he is away from the bucket, a classmate is allowed to take balls out and throw them back onto the floor. Can Mario get all the balls into the bucket?
- Much of the business will be mimed, but consider using a real broom.

Chapters

Dividing the scene into chapters will help your actor to navigate through **Timothy**'s actions and thoughts.

A chapter begins when Timothy's focus is drawn to something new. Give each chapter a title. The first, in which Timothy is primarily focusing on his Dad, ends with 'I'll try here' and might be called 'Getting off the Train.' The second, in which Timothy's prime focus is the magazine, runs until the children push him and might be called 'Tintin'.

Project Work

- CHARACTER WORKSHEET
- KNOWLEDGE NOTES
- STAGE DIAGRAM
- RESEARCH: Hot climate
- OBSERVATION: Feeling hot
- OUTING: Train station in rush hour
- ART: Umbrella woman

GLOSSARY

restless	swipe	desperation
stall	swerve	aimless
scramble	weave	

Other Characters

Your actor will have to work hard to evoke the crowded French platform and to manage the frequent switches of focus in this scene. If you have a class, use stand-ins for Dad, the group of children, the man Timothy treads on, the woman with the umbrella and the crowd that gathers round.

Work chapter by chapter. Stage each one with stand-ins; remove them when Timothy has a fixed idea of where they are and what they are doing.

Engage your stand-ins in the creation of the scene so that they commit to it and help to create its very busy atmosphere. Even when not playing a particular character, they can move around the stage as part of the crowd.

Dad might need a couple of short lines, which can be improvised or scripted by Timothy. The trodden-on man might voice his displeasure. The umbrella woman and other crowd members think Timothy is a thief and should tell him so – in French. Timothy hasn't a clue what they are saying, so it could be angry gobbledegook French.

Hot and Bothered

Timothy has been stuck in his seat on the train for a long time. He is hot and thirsty. It's even hotter on the platform than it was on the train. The platform is crowded, and tempers are likely to be short.

Playing the scene against a soundtrack of a busy station will help Timothy imagine his surroundings. Turn up the volume from time to time, so that he has to raise his voice to make himself heard. You could record your own soundtrack or search in YouTube for one that's free to use (try 'busy train station audio').

What happens to the body when we overheat?:

- High energy and tension would heat us up even more, so we try to reduce effort in our movements. We are loose and floppy.
- Our forehead sweats – we wipe it dry to stop sweat dripping into our eyes and making them sting.

- Sweaty clothes stick uncomfortably to our bodies – we unstick them and fan air across our skin.
- We become irritable.

GAME: RAISING THE TEMPERATURE

Ask your students to walk around the space in neutral. Explain that you are going to raise the temperature one degree at a time from zero to ten, at which point it is so hot that it becomes impossible to move, and they flop to the ground under a shady tree to sleep. They are allowed to interact (but no contact). So they can complain, scold, insult and ignore all they like.

Work up through the numbers, leaving plenty of space in between for students to absorb the change and express it through the body.

0. Cool dudes
1. Wafts of warmth
2. Here comes the sun
3. Prickles of sweat
4. Sticky clothes
5. Hot and bothered
6. Heavy limbs
7. Need… water!
8. Getting angry
9. Sizzling Sahara
10. Too Hot to Handle!

Develop this exercise into a guessing game using numbered cards. A student picks a card at random and walks across the stage at the appropriate level of hotness. Others guess the number.

Consolidate by asking Timothy where he thinks the temperature of this scene is and reminding him always to play at that level.

Obstacle Course

Despite the heat, this scene is high tempo, and Timothy will need pace and a flustered energy in his delivery. He simply wants to find an ice cream, but there are several obstacles in his way, and time is very short.

Set up a real obstacle course so that your actor can read the scene while clambering over chairs, under tables and through hula hoops against the stopwatch.

Timothy not only fails to get the ice cream but also fails to make it back to the train in time. You could offer a prize if your actor completes the course in time but blow the whistle (signalling that time is up) before he gets to the end. He might feel as disappointed, frustrated and upset as Timothy feels at the end of the scene. Poor Timothy. If he's acting the scene well, give him his prize anyway after putting him through all this suffering!

Game: Gobbledegook Crisis

The French bystanders accuse Timothy of stealing. He tries to protest his innocence but cannot make himself understood. Practise this exasperating situation with a quick game.

Write or type some crisis situations on pieces of paper and jumble them up. Two actors stand at opposite sides of the stage. One picks a crisis and must communicate it to the other. He can mime, move, and speak – but not in English. Can the other actor work out what the problem is?

Crisis situations are useful for quick games and improvisations. Examples can be downloaded from the web page which accompanies this book.

Penguin Character

There is plenty of penguin footage your actor can watch, either in class or at home (see page 9 for a note on online research). Have a look at nature documentaries, of which there are numerous excerpts on YouTube. You could watch the highly rated 2005 documentary *March of the Penguins.*

Project Work

- CHARACTER WORKSHEET
- KNOWLEDGE NOTES
- STAGE DIAGRAM
- RESEARCH: *Penguins*
- OUTING: *Zoo*
- ART: *Advert for the contest*
- WRITING: *Wild animal songs*

GLOSSARY

compère	famine	proceedings
handmike	dignity	vanish
ambition	unemployment	

Observe the way a penguin moves its head, wings and feet. How do they hold themselves when standing still? How do they walk slowly and quickly? How do they engage with and respond to one another? React to threats and dangers? Express happiness? Where is their centre of gravity?

Ask your actor to take the stage and penguinise one part of his body – his arms can become wings, for example. How is his movement affected? He still needs to do human things. How will he pick things up? Scratch his head?

Work on other body parts and find the combination that makes him penguinish. Ask him to move around the space until he gets comfortable in his penguin skin. Help him to locate his penguin 'centre' – which part of his body leads his movement? Where does his energy radiate from?

Explore what voice such an animal might produce. Ask him to mill around the room, introduce himself (to you or classmates), comment on the weather, talk about his plans for the day and so on. Students who join in the

❈ A HAPPY EXAMINER ❈

*I*t's hard work – physically and mentally – being a LAMDA examiner. Look after your examiner, so that he or she can focus on giving your students the best possible exam experience.

Make sure your students have clean copies of both scripts (Acting Anthology and own-choice). These should be typed in a large font with lines well spaced. Leave out stage directions, so that the examiner can check the lines at a glance and spend as much time as possible watching the performance. Make sure your students know exactly what to do from the moment they enter until the moment they leave the exam room and can easily manage props, costumes and chairs.

If you are running a private centre, treat your examiner as a special guest. Plan the day thoroughly so that it runs like clockwork. Draft in stewards. Give the examiner a comfortable chair and a large adult-height desk. Maintain a good temperature in the room – your examiner will be sitting still in it for a whole day. Provide plenty of water. In the breaks, offer tea, coffee, juice and biscuits. Give some thought to lunch, an important break for you and the examiner.

At the end of the day, ask for feedback about your centre in general and about how you ran the day. If there is anything that can be improved, do it in time for the next session!

milling exercise, particularly those playing animal characters in other scenes – can work in character. If you have enough animals, set up a zoo.

It might be fun to have a look at other penguin performances. The villainous Penguin, played by Burgess Meredith in the 1960s TV series *Batman* and Danny DeVito in the 1992 film *Batman Returns,* is a penguinised human. You might find inspiration, too, from humanised penguins, such as Pingu and Feathers McGraw from the first Wallace and Gromit film, *The Wrong Trousers* (1993).

Kingsley

Character work should extend beyond **Debit**'s penguinness. What else is there to say about Kingsley Debit?

- His status is high: he gives instructions, sets the rules and controls proceedings. He is authoritative (there is no apparent disquiet or dissent among the animals he is talking to).
- He is in work mode.
- He has the charm and charisma one would expect from a TV host.
- His presenting style is upbeat, energetic and full of superlatives.

Setting

The scene is set in a TV dressing room. Invite ideas about the location. It might have mirrors surrounded by lights, a sink, good luck cards, flowers, a clothes rail and so on. The action takes place behind the scenes at a major prime-time TV show, so Kinglsey might want to add some glitz and glamour.

Apart from Debit and a golden eagle named Quilla, there are several other animals, referred to by Debit as 'the rest of you'. Decide how many contestants there are on the show and rehearse the scene with stand-ins, so that Debit has an idea of who he is addressing and when.

Place everything, including the camera/screen Debit talks into at the end, in such a way that your actor faces front and shares his performance.

The Contest

There are six ground rules to the Wild Animal Song Contest. Ask your actor to commit the rules to memory and explain them in his own words. Put him in the hot seat and ask him why the rules are important. If they are broken, what are the consequences? Have they been broken in the past? What happened? Talk more generally about the show, about what he is looking for in a winning contestant and about the worst performance he has ever seen.

If you have time, stage a round of the TV show. If other students are playing animal characters in other scenes, they can enter in character. Otherwise, they can pick an animal. Ask them to write a short song appropriate to their animal. If this idea is daunting, allow them to adapt the words of a familiar tune, such as Twinkle Twinkle or Happy Birthday.

Depending on your class size, you can also appoint judges (your students may draw inspiration from *Britain's Got Talent* or *Strictly Come Dancing*). The judges can interview the contestants before they perform and give their assessments afterwards (without being too negative or insulting).

Character

This stand-alone scene leaves the actor quite free to create **Natalie**'s back story. First mine the text to draw out the facts:

- Her parents are divorced.
- She is about to meet her dad's new girlfriend for the first time.
- She wants to make a good impression because it is important to her dad – this is the first of his girlfriends he has asked her to meet.
- She has asked her friend to help her decide what to wear.

Project Work
- CHARACTER WORKSHEET
- KNOWLEDGE NOTES
- STAGE DIAGRAM
- RESEARCH: Natalie's playlist
- ART: Picture or collage of Natalie
- WRITING: Diary entry; friend's lines

GLOSSARY

good impression	mumble
impending	shuffle
stepmother	

You can then make judgements about Natalie's feelings and state of mind:

- She loves her dad and wants to make him happy.
- She is anxious about this meeting.
- She is frustrated by her friend's failure to help.
- She is worried that her dad's girlfriend will not like her.
- The thought of her dad remarrying had not occurred to her before.

From this basis, your actor can invent a full biography for Natalie. There are all sorts of ways to develop a character's back story:

- Fill in a character worksheet (such as our downloadable example).
- Draw Natalie (and annotate the picture).
- Go through old magazines and cut out pictures for a collage – faces, animals, places, possessions or anything else that suggests a connection with the character. As with all artistic work, the process (and the discussion afterwards) are more important than how 'good' the result is.
- Imagine that the meeting with the stepmother has just happened and write a diary entry describing it.
- Make a playlist of Natalie's favourite songs.

Hot-seating will consolidate this work. Ask questions with straightforward answers before delving into Natalie's inner life, past history and the present situation. Decisions about the friend can be made by Natalie alone or in collaboration with a student who will stand in during rehearsals. The stand-in can work with Natalie on scripting lines or interjections for the friend.

You could hot seat Natalie in situ and ask her for a guided tour of the location (Natalie's bedroom?). Ask detailed questions about furniture, décor and possessions and establish her emotional connection to the space.

Situation: A Jumble of Feelings

Look again at the judgements you made about Natalie's feelings and state of mind and ask your actor to turn them into 'I' statements:

- I love my father and want him to be happy.
- I am anxious about meeting my stepmother.

Encapsulate each statement in a single emotion word: loving, anxious, frustrated and so on. Ask your actor to make a tableau (frozen picture) or invent a gesture that expresses each emotion. Encourage bold, even abstract shapes. Commit them to memory and test them – write the words on cards; the actor picks a card and strikes the pose; you (or classmates) guess which word it was.

Go back to the text; find moments where each of the 'I' statements arises as the dominant emotion and see if the actor can incorporate each pose or gesture into a performance of the scene.

From a pile of felt-tips, ask your actor to choose the colour that matches each emotion. Decorate a copy of the script with these colours, making clear visual distinctions between sections where different emotions predominate.

The Changing Stepmother

Natalie imagines two contrasting versions of the imminent meeting:
- My Dad is going to marry a beautiful princess and I must dazzle her. I will wear my best clothes and be on my best behaviour.
- My Dad is going to marry an evil witch and I must make a terrible impression. I will be scruffy, I will mumble and I will shuffle my feet.

Both outcomes are vivid in Natalie's imagination. If you have a class, improvise each imagined scene with classmates playing Dad and the stepmother. Exaggerate the chocolate box perfection on the one hand and the fairytale horribleness on the other. If you don't have a group, Natalie can bring each stepmother to life in a solo improvisation.

Natalie's image of her stepmother starts positively, but the idea of an evil witch gradually takes hold. As a physical warm-up for Natalie or a whole group, transform from princess to witch over a count of ten. Encourage students to commit the whole body to the characterisations. Are the witch's toes curled? Are the princess's ears perky?

If Natalie starts this scene at level 1 ('my stepmother is a princess') and ends at 10 ('my stepmother is a witch'), can she chart her journey in numbers? Does she progress gradually or in leaps? She can annotate a copy of the script with numbers. Then recruit a classmate to play (silently) the character Natalie is imagining, transforming from the princess at the beginning of the scene to the witch at the end. You or another student can follow the numbered script and hold up cards to indicate the transformation.

You could also bring Natalie's journey to life by using classmates as the two contrasting stepmothers. Place them at opposite sides of the room. Natalie starts close to the princess and moves away as she becomes confused and worried by the thought of having another mother. Then, as the idea of an evil stepmother arises, the witch crosses to her and pulls her slowly across to the other side of the room. Does Natalie resist the witch's pull? When might she turn to confront the witch?

In a solo class, use pictures on the wall; Natalie controls her own journey.

The final section involves a strong decision: I must prevent my Dad from marrying this woman. Natalie triumphs over the imaginary evil stepmother. She can push the witch to the ground or rip the the picture off the wall.

NEVER COULD SAY GOODBYE

by Nick Teed ✼ *Acting Anthology page 121*

Setting

Set the scene by starting with the facts. It is summer, and fine enough for golf. There is a shed and a garden bench. **Harriet** is outside the shed but talks to her friend, who is inside. Harriet must also be able to see inside. Her focus switches from the shed to her memories and back again to the shed. All the time, she should be angled towards the front. From when she sits on the bench until close to the end of the scene, Harriet is lost in her memories, so she needn't face the shed.

> ### Project Work
> - CHARACTER WORKSHEET
> - KNOWLEDGE NOTES
> - STAGE DIAGRAM
> - RESEARCH: *Evacuees*
> - OUTING: *Garden on a summer's day*
> - ART: *Key images – collage, scrap book, spider diagram or thought slideshow*
> - WRITING: *Memory of Grandpa*
> - GLOSSARY
>
> clutter   evacuee
>
> abandoned

Prompted by you, Harriet should imagine other aspects of the setting.

- How big is the garden?
- Is it very lush and well planted?
- Are there birds and other animals?
- What can you hear? What can you smell?
- How far away is the back of the house?
- Who is in the house? Can they be seen?
- Is the shed rickety or solid?

Go into as much detail as time allows. A richly painted foreground of sights, sounds and smells will give Harriet a focus whenever she drifts out of her memories and back to the here and now. The more decisions she makes, the greater will be her sense of ownership of the performance.

A warm Sunday in a familiar garden has a special atmosphere and rhythm. The mood of the scene is melancholy, wistful and tender. Can Harriet imagine herself into the setting and let the words wash through her?

Mental Images

Harriet's first words are comments on the smell of damp wood and the old paint pots. She speculates that Ayesha's grandfather is a busy man. Next she looks at all the clutter. She speculates that the grandfather is a hoarder. Then she reflects on old people more generally.

The scene follows this pattern throughout: Harriet moves from something observed, usually something visual (or a memory of something visual) to pondering. Her recollection of her own grandfather begins with cobwebs and spiders and moves on to his inability to throw things away.

Visual snapshots are scattered throughout the scene – kissing Gran goodbye; talking to the nurse outside the ward; the evacuee waving from the train; letters posted home. Help your actor to form clear pictures in her own mind. Strong mental images can be very powerful in performance and may help your actor to transport herself into her character's world.

Pick around ten images that you both agree are crucial to the scene. Draw them, take photographs, or cut pictures out of magazines. Harriet can look at them during rehearsal; she can make a collage or page for a scrap book or a mind map; or use them for a thought slideshow (see box).

Grandpa to Grandpa

What exactly stimulates Harriet's memories of her own grandfather? The shed? The word *clutter*? Is it the thought of Ayesha's grandfather complaining when he finds the shed tidy – would Harriet's grandfather have done the same? Was there a time when he was angry at things being tidy? Did he hate tidiness? Is it something about the garden? Does she remember a similar summer Sunday when her grandfather was alive? When she thinks of her grandfather, does she smile? Or feel sad? Or both at the same time, or first one and then the other? What breed was the dog?

Ask as many questions as you think your actor can handle, and make sure that the answers are not just casually thrown around but are decisions that become owned and embedded in the performance. Every decision brings with it an extra sprinkle of truthfulness. The image of Grandpa surreptitiously slipping a lead around the neck of a Yorkshire terrier will have a subtly different impact from the image of him doing the same to an Alsatian.

Further Idea

This scene offers several opportunities to improvise episodes that are mentioned or described:

- saying goodbye to Gran
- visiting Grandpa at the hospital
- the evacuee waves goodbye to his mother as the train leaves.

After students have improvised the scenes, give Harriet a few moments with the cast to direct and rerun them. If time allows, you might invent one or more further Grandpa scenes to improvise.

❋ THOUGHT SLIDESHOW ❋

*Y*ou can bring intensity to a reflective scene by looking at its images. Find the key images and bring them to life by drawing them, taking photographs or cutting pictures out of magazines. For this scene, you might collect together images of:

• an old shed	• cobwebs and spiders	• a bombed house
• a cluttered shelf	• an old woman	• a man with his family
• an old man	• a hospital or a nurse	
• a very tidy shelf	• a departing train carrying evacuees away	

Get your pictures onto a laptop or tablet and make a slideshow. With your actor, decide where in the scene each image arises in her mind. Then operate the slideshow for her to watch as she speaks the words. Make sure she absorbs and engages with each image.

If the scene is densely packed with imagery, choose only the key images. Allow time for each image to settle in the mind before the next one is called up.

When you take the physical images away, does their imprint remain?

A MAPLE LEAF WONDER
by Clare Price ✳ *Acting Anthology page 123*

An Imaginary Mess

There is a great deal of elaborate business in this scene; done with skill and strong characterisation, it would work well as a mimed scene. Spend time with the script to one side, working on the business. First list all **Suzie**'s actions:

- Break four eggs into bowl
- Mix with hands
- Get tin opener, spreading mess over worktop
- Open tin of peaches
- Mix peaches in with hands
- Pour in nutmeg (first a little, then the whole jar)
- Place slices of bread around baking tray
- Pour peach mixture in
- Set cooker…

… and so on. Continue until you have the story of the scene.

The actions are complicated and the environment is full of tricky objects. Each of the main actions listed above needs to be broken down into its component stages. For example:

- Set cooker =>
  - Look at cooker
  - Notice cooker is not switched on – react!
  - Decide to extend cooking time to 30 minutes

✳ MIME ✳

*M*ake time for mime work in your LAMDA exam classes. Even if you don't have students taking a mime exam, it's an essential part of the actor's toolkit, especially when performing under exam or festival conditions with little in the way of props and furniture.

Raid your props cupboard for objects of various weights. Let your students observe what happens in their hands and arms when they handle the objects. Mime each object in turn – pick it up, put it down and pass it from hand to hand. Teach the concept of object permanence – if they put something down, they must pick it up from the same spot. If they pick up a new object, have they put the other one down first, or has it just evaporated? Pass the mimed objects around the circle: are you convinced by the transference of weight from one person to the next?

Set up tasks that require different degrees of effort. Ask them to observe their own and each other's bodies as they tear paper, pull apart magnets and unscrew a stiff jar lid.

Your students will probably express effort on the face. Facial expressions can help an audience understand what is going on physically and emotionally in a mimed scene. Teach your students the importance of approach before take; instead of just seeing an object and picking it up, they should see it, react to it (express an emotion towards it) and then pick it up.

- Turn temperature dial on cooker
- Notice cooker has now started to get warm

It is unlikely that bread, peaches and nutmeg are kept in the same cupboard, so you need to separate these out and decide exactly where in the kitchen each one lives. How high up are the cupboards? What kinds of handles do they have? Do they bang when you push them shut? How much bread is left in the packet? There is almost no limit to the detail you can go into.

You might have a student who enjoys getting everything written down in a notebook and finds this the best way of learning and remembering her actions. Or your student might not be a keen writer and might have excellent muscle memory, learning best through physical repetition. Find the best way of detailing all the business and committing it to memory.

When everything is worked out, the original list of actions can serve to cue your actor through the sequence. Stick it on a wall for her to read from or prompt her by reading out each action in the sequence.

REFINING

When you are refining the work, ask your actor to perform in slow motion so that you can both check on her precision. Can the audience see a clear distinction between objects of different sizes and weights, so that everyone is clear when she is holding a jar of nutmeg, a baking tray or an apron? Is Suzie obeying the basic rules of object permanence, so that a thing keeps its size and weight all the while she is holding it, stays in her hands until she puts it down, and is picked up from wherever it was put down?

Test Suzie's mime skills with a quiz game: imagine that all the objects that feature in the scene are spread out on a table on the stage. Suzie fetches one and 'shows' it to the audience. Can they work out what it is?

Facial expressions will be important throughout the scene; pay particular attention to the moments where things don't quite go to plan: the obstinacy of the flour, the sticky mess on the worktop, the lumpiness of the mixture, the cold oven and so on. Look for other strong reactions – the cloud of flour and the moment when she hears her mother return, for example.

If you have a suitable room, consider practising once with real ingredients. You could cover the table and floor in polythene dust sheets (and warn Suzie to wear clothes that she doesn't mind getting mucky!).

Further Ideas

Make time for character work. Your actor can make decisions about Suzie's age, family and school life. She should also make decisions about Suzie's personality. Is she scatty or organised? Energetic or calm? Self-confident or self-doubting? Imagine that these and other opposite pairs are at either end of a scale that stretches across the room. Read out each pair; Suzie stands wherever on the scale she feels her character belongs.

Suzie is fantasising about being a TV chef. Things don't quite go to plan. But what is the fantasy? Ask Suzie to improvise a version of the scene in which the cooking goes perfectly. She might cook a different recipe.

Map out the kitchen – include doors, windows, the sink, the fridge and so on. Where is the the front door to the house?

Source

This scene has been adapted from the first chapter ('The Egg') of E Nesbit's 1904 children's novel. There are some departures from the source episode, and some work has been done to extract the **Phoenix**'s lines from the narrative. If your student reads the original, he will get a sense of the circumstances, the setting and the different characters of the children.

Character

You could develop a character for Phoenix from various starting points:

HE'S SMOKIN' HOT

Phoenix has just emerged from the flames and is radiating heat. How might his movement be affected? Explore fieriness with the following exercise:

- Ask your actor for words to describe how flames move (they flicker, sway and dance, for example). Accept sound words, such as crackle and roar.
- He begins by curling himself up on the floor, as though he were a pile of logs. You play some music and pretend to light the logs.
- The fire starts gradually. It grows as the music gets louder until it is burning fully. As the music fades, the flames slowly die down until the fire is burnt out and there is just a pile of ash.
- Use this exercise as a group warm-up. Afterwards, students can choose a fire creature – phoenix, salamander, dragon, scorpion, chimera – and incorporate fieriness into their physicality as they move around the space.

If you work with stand-ins for the children in the scene, can they feel the heat whenever Phoenix moves close to them? If Phoenix plays off their reactions – by being apologetic or confused, say – the children will be present in the scene even when you remove the stand-ins from the stage.

What happens to Phoenix's movements as he cools down? Is he more or less comfortable when he's hot? Does he move more or less freely?

HE'S A THOUSAND-YEAR OLD BABY

One moment Phoenix was in a wilderness. Then two thousand years have passed and he finds himself in the basement of a London house. Use another movement exercise to explore the experience of hatching into a new world.

- Your actor walks freely around the space. He imagines that he is somewhere outdoors, far away and a long time ago.
- He finds a space, lies down and curls up tightly as though inside an egg.
- Play some music; when he hears it, he slowly hatches out of his egg, keeping eyes tightly closed until the end. He makes a crack in the shell

Project Work

- CHARACTER WORKSHEET
- KNOWLEDGE NOTES
- STAGE DIAGRAM
- RESEARCH: Flames; eagles
- OBSERVATION: Seeing things anew
- WRITING: Encyclopedia entry

GLOSSARY

liven up	ornithology	acquire
symbol	fabulous	feverish
aromatic	antiquity	enchanter
mantelpiece	whirr	worth
emerge	reside	gum
debtor	weary	cornice
flattering	monotony	

and slowly stretches toes and fingers. He unlocks ankles, knees, wrists and elbows. He gradually begins to uncurl. He lifts his head and opens his eyes.

- First he explores the room just with his eyes. He looks at the strange and unfamiliar surfaces, materials and objects. What does he notice? How much time has passed? Ten years? Ten thousand years?
- He gets up, moves slowly around the space and inspects his surroundings. What is most interesting or unusual?
- Exhausted by the new information, when the music fades he sits to rest.
- Discuss how Phoenix might have a newborn quality in performance.

Although he is newly hatched, Phoenix is also old and wise. He corrects the mistakes in the encyclopaedia and talks with authority about himself and the world. He is a magical creature, and when the sound of a key is heard in the lock, he immediately knows what it is and how to respond.

Can your actor reconcile these contradictions in Phoenix's character?

HE'S A BIRD

Phoenixes are often depicted as eagle-like. Look at photos of eagles or videos of them in motion (on the ground rather than in the air). How do they move their wings, feet, head and eyes? Practise moving around the room as an eagle.

HE'S A GROWN-UP

The Phoenix is somewhat schoolmasterly in the way he addresses the children. He considers himself their intellectual superior. He uses long words. He tells stories, but with the aim of educating rather than entertaining and in the certainty that he will be listened to uninterrupted. He is self-assured and fond of his own appearance.

Further Ideas

- Improvise the ending of the Phoenix's previous life. Divide your class into groups of three (Phoenix, prince and princess). Ask for a scene that includes some dialogue and some exciting physical action.
- Find opportunities for the Phoenix to respond and react to the other characters. Look for the impulse to speak the next line, so that it does not sound like a prepared speech. Which line is addressed to which child? How does the age of each child affect how he speaks to them?

❊ USING MUSIC ❊

*M*usic can play a valuable role even in 'straight acting' classes. When students are working on their own (learning lines, drawing, project work), some gentle instrumental music in the background creates a studious atmosphere. In movement exercises, music helps students to become absorbed and encourages adventurous, abstract and spontaneous movement.

Avoid vocals, as the aim is to switch off (rather than engage) the busy, linguistic part of the brain. Unless the exercise calls for it, avoid hectically up-tempo music. Ballet music is an excellent background to energetic movement work. Electronic music and orchestral film soundtracks provide a range of atmospheres, from the rural to the robotic. Calm a class down with yoga and meditation music.

Set up your music before the class and make sure you don't need to be online to play it. A list of recommended tracks is available on the web page which accompanies this book.

Context

This scene has been adapted from an English translation (1975) of a Swedish children's novel published in 1973. It is a fantastical and at times breathless adventure story but also has a melancholy undercurrent with meditations on death and the afterlife.

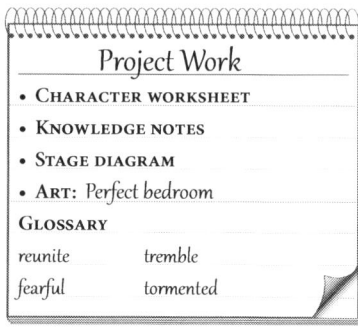

Project Work
- CHARACTER WORKSHEET
- KNOWLEDGE NOTES
- STAGE DIAGRAM
- ART: *Perfect bedroom*
- GLOSSARY

reunite	*tremble*
fearful	*tormented*

There is a resistance movement in the neighbouring area (Thorn Rose Valley) against the fearsome Tengil, who has seized control there. **Rusky** lives in Cherry Valley, where Sofia leads a secret group in support of the Thorn Rose Valley resistance. Jonathan has gone to Thorn Rose Valley with her blessing. Rusky knows she will think him too young to join his brother.

Bringing it to Life

The adaptation is almost verbatim, and there is little dialogue or interaction. To prevent the performance from straying towards a prose reading, boost the drama with strong characterisation and movement and a commitment to the setting. Identify and emphasise the points of high emotion and conflict.

THE SETTING

Nangiyala is a verison of paradise, so your actor can create his perfect bedroom. What is in the room besides a bed? What kinds of curtains or shutters are there and how do they close and open? How high is the ceiling? What decorates the walls? Outside, what is the garden like? How many rabbits are there and what is their hutch like? What is the weather like in Nangiyala?

When you have established the two settings, spend some time moving around them. Rusky can give you (or classmates) a guided tour (see page 57).

SHOWING AND TELLING

When you come back to the script, ask another student to narrate slowly while Rusky acts out the scene in silence. Encourage him to move as much as possible and to commit to the moments of high drama – waking terrified; feeling frightened and lonely; deciding to go in search of his brother.

Repeat the exercise with the actors switched around to explore different ways of coordinating the telling and the showing. When should the narration drive the scene, and when should the action have priority? Are there opportunities to show before telling? Take the first line, for example. Rusky might begin the scene by silently establishing the setting (making his room ready for a night's sleep). He shivers with cold and then speaks the first words as he gets into bed. In this way, the narration supports rather than dictates the action. Could the action come first elsewhere?

At moments of very sudden drama, the showing and the telling might go together, so that at the end of the scene, Rusky bangs his hand hard on the rabbit hutch just as he says the word 'banged'.

You could put the script aside and experiment with ways of showing and telling. Ask another student to take the stage and silently act out a short, dramatic scene. Rusky watches and narrates the scene in the first person.

- Your grandmother's cat is stuck up a tree. You sneak away to transform into Birdman, your superhero alter-ego, and return to save the day.
- You wake up in the middle of the night and realise that you've forgotten it's your Mum's birthday tomorrow. You sneak out to the local 24-hour shop to buy her a present.

EMOTIONS RUNNING HIGH

At various points Rusky is terrified, in a frenzy, desperate, lonely, confused and tormented. These emotions should not just be described but expressed through the body, face and voice. Write each emotion down on a piece of paper and ask him to create a tableau for each, with the whole body engaged. Then jumble up the pieces of paper and ask him to pick one, take the stage and strike the pose. Can you (or classmates) identify the emotion?

Go back to the text and work out where each emotion arises. Can Rusky include each tableau as he works through the scene? Refine the poses so that they arise naturally and are integrated into the flow of the text.

THE NEED TO SPEAK

Rusky has no idea when he starts speaking that he will carry on for five paragraphs. Every new idea needs a fresh impulse, and the actor should always be speaking in response or reaction to something.

In some scenes, the stimulus to speak is quite obvious – something happens, the character sees something or another character does something. Here, the stimulus is not so obvious. You can provide one by playing an opposing voice, continually questioning, doubting, disagreeing and objecting. This will give your actor something to push back against.

Stand to one side and speak quietly, as though you are a nagging internal voice. Be sceptical, negative and dismissive of everything your actor says:

The next morning…	*What did you do?*
I sat for hours…	*All on your own?!*
out with my rabbits…	*Did you sing to them?*
and thought about what I should do.	*Why didn't you just talk to someone?*
I had no one to talk to, no one to ask.	

With this sort of insistent questioning, you give your actor an impulse to speak and turn a solo scene into one half of a conversation.

Further Ideas

- One way of varying the pace of this scene would be to decide when Rusky's heart is beating fast and to move and speak with greater energy at those moments (and to slow down speech and movement at other moments).
- Breathe fresh life into the performance by asking Rusky to deliver it to different imaginary audiences – a young child, his favourite aunt or uncle, a policeman and so on.

DOLPHIN SUMMER

adapted by LAMDA from Monica Edwards ✳ *Acting Anthology page 131*

Source Text

This scene has been faithfully adapted from a children's novel of 1963, one of the *Romney Marsh* series.

Location

The location – and the way **Rissa** and **Tamzin** respond to it – contributes much to the scene's atmosphere. Spend time with your actors imagining the location and exploring how to bring it to life.

- **MINE THE TEXT**
  Start with the facts – list everything the text tells you about the setting:
  - Romney Marsh, Sussex
  - Empty except for sheep
  - Path
  - Net sheds
  - River
  - Warm moonlit/starry night
  - Stones on the beach
  - Lowish tide; warm water

- **RESEARCH (ONLINE)**
  The writer, drawing on memories of her childhood, has set this scene somewhere real. Your actors can search for online photos of Romney Marsh beaches, in quiet time or as homework. If one image does not provide an exact model for the location, make a collage that includes pictures of net sheds, a shingle beach and other features of the setting.

- **RESEARCH (SITE VISIT)**
  If your actors live near a beach, a research visit (ideally together) will have immeasurable value whenever they have to imagine themselves out of a brightly lit drama room and onto a moonlit seashore.

  At the beach, they should close their eyes and absorb the smells, sounds and textures of the location: listen to the waves, gulp the air, walk barefoot across pebbles, find a rope, paddle in the sea.

  They can take photographs and collect small items whose smell or texture is evocative. The foraged items can be included in a collage, scrap book or display.

  In their notebooks, they can jot down any words that spring to mind, as a list, on a spider diagram or in a paragraph or poem.

- **SET THE STAGE**
  Next, work with your actors to map out the scene. Establish the route the girls take:

  Path > net shed > beach > water's edge > deeper > back to shore

  It is not easy to stage a scene with several locations, especially in a small playing space. The key choice is how to draw the line that goes from beach to deep water (and eventually to France). It could run across the stage, up-to-down or down-to-up. However you map it, do so in a way that allows both girls to share their performance with the examiner.

If your drama room is small, instead of having the girls move from place to place through the scene, let the different locations come to them. With this approach, the actors must use strong body language to express clear differences between path, beach and water. Explore how you might mark the transition from one place to the next – a few steps on the spot? One very clear step? A change of orientation?

- Consolidate all your work on the setting with a stage diagram.

In the Water

Your girls' physical acting skills are put to the test when they move from beach to water and from wading to swimming. Make sure they observe themselves next time they go for a swim.

There should be a physical response when the first wave laps over the feet. Then work out a way of wading convincingly. The whole leg is engaged in a movement that begins from the hips. Practise the muscular release when the girls' feet leave the seabed and they are swimming. What facial expression might signal the moment when the shoulders go under the water? Are the girls swimming or treading water? How do their arms move?

Tamzin disappears soundlessly from view (Rissa doesn't notice). She could drop quickly to the floor and curl up into a ball.

Ponies

Cascade and Siani are very present in the first third of the scene. Having two actors stand in will help Tamzin and Rissa work out their points of focus when their attention is on the ponies. (If you have an actor doing the Black Beauty Grade 3 solo scene, you have one ready-made horse.)

Spend some time imagining what the ponies looks like and how they behave. What colour are they? How big are they? Where are their heads in relation to the girls' heads? Are they calm or jittery?

If either actor (or anyone in the class) has been around horses, ask her to describe what it is like to lead and tie up a pony. She can act it out as she describes it. Otherwise, your actors can do some research by looking at videos online or even by visiting stables.

Interplay

The preamble states that 'Rissa is practical and Tamzin is dreamy'. Is this accurate? Ask each actor to find things they say or do that supports this view. Is there anything that contradicts it?

Work on the relationship, too. Can each actor find something the other character says or does that:

- surprises her • is typical • amuses her • irritates her • scares her?

Follow up by asking each actor to give a short presentation in which she describes her friend. Alternatively, ask each actor to draw the other character and annotate the drawing. If time allows, you can explore the history of their friendship more deeply (see pages 76–77 for ideas).

STOWAWAYS

by Jacqueline Emery ✳ *Acting Anthology page134*

The First Day of the Rest of My Life

Emma and **Lily**'s lives have converged in this place and at this moment, a turning point for both of them. Each has a very different past behind them and a very different future ahead of them (or so they imagine). Work with both actors on exploring first their characters' past life and then their future dreams.

- Start by establishing the facts of each character's life up to this point. The girls have run away because they were unhappy with life as it was; what was making them unhappy?
- You could consolidate this work in a number of ways:
  - Your actors take the hot seat and answer questions about their past life.
  - They pick the five or six key events from their life (the last would be seeing the advertisement for this journey) and draw a comic strip illustrating these moments.
  - They tell the story of their life in a series of tableaux (frozen pictures). Classmates can be recruited as the other characters in each girl's life. These tableaux could be developed into short improvised scenes.
  - They pick a prop that they imagine relates to a significant incident in their past and tell you the story of that prop.
- Next work with your actors on the future that they imagine awaits them. They were not only pushed onto this ship by their unhappy lives, they were pulled onto it by the prospect of a better life elsewhere. What will that life be like? There are several ways of exploring this idea:
  - Again, your actors take the hot seat and answer questions about their hopes and dreams.
  - They draw a picture or make a collage of the gold-paved New York they imagine.
  - They improvise a scene in which they meet up again five years later. Everything has worked out just as each girl dreamed it would.
  - This would be a good moment to discuss the irony of the scene (everyone knows how this journey really ends).

FOLLOW-UP

A nice private study task (in class or at home) would be to draw the advertisement that gave the girls the idea of stowing away on the *Titanic*. You could also search online for images of real adverts for the *Titanic* or other ocean liners.

The Here and Now

Both girls find themselves cast adrift in unfamiliar surroundings. Establish the geography and conditions of the setting and work on the girls' attitudes to their surroundings.

THE TRUNK ROOM

The scene is set in a room full of boxes, suitcases and trunks. The space is likely to be functional rather than smart. Decide whether it is hot or cold down there and what noises might be heard – the ship's engines? Creaking timbers? Sounds of the sea? Is it close or airy?

Circumstances do not allow for piles of boxes on the stage. If possible, both girls should have something to hide behind, even if it is only a stack of chairs or an upturned table. It is important for the opening of the scene that Emma does not know Lily is there; also, the hiding establishes an atmosphere of mischief and secrecy. In the absence of furniture, each girl can enter the scene from the wings as though she has been hiding.

STOWAWAYS

Hiding is thrilling. It can also be nerve-wracking and terrifying if being found means serious danger. If your drama room (or any outdoor space you have access to) allows for it, play a game of hide-and-seek with your students as a fun warm-up – and follow up by asking them to describe the experience of hiding. Alternatively (and if you have a group), play a blindfold version:

- Students form a circle around the edge of a flat space free from obstacles.
- Two students in the middle are blindfolded. Spin them around so they are disorientated. Set a time limit within which one (the hunter) has to catch the other (the prey).
- Players will need to listen carefully for breaths, rustles and floorboard creaks. Those in the circle form a safe buffer by holding their hands up in front of them, palms out.

While hearts are still racing, go straight into the scene.

Other Ideas: Lurches

The ship lurches three times; practice until the timing is perfect and both girls are falling (or nearly falling) at the same time. They should act as though they have been given a sharp push. In rehearsal, they could work on getting the correct movement by actually pushing each other (see page 71).

✳ HOT SEATING (2) ✳

*T*ry different methods of hot seating. Your actor needn't even sit; ideas might flow more readily if she's on her feet and free to move around. Give her pens and paper and let her doodle while she talks to you. Place her in the scene's location and ask her to describe her surroundings to you. Or interview her for a newspaper or on a TV chat show.

Start with factual questions, then deepen the work by asking about circumstances and feelings that lie beyond the scope of the script.

Allow consolidation time after the exercise. Through discussion or note-taking, firm up the decisions. Return to the script and see how those decisions affect the playing of the scene.

Hot seating can also be done in pairs or groups. For more ideas, see page 10.

COME ON!
by Kenneth Pickering ❋ *Acting Anthology page 138*

Character Contrasts

The drama in this scene, as with many of the duologues, derives from two contrasting attitudes to the same situation. Mine the differences between the two characters. First explore ways in which the same action may be performed very differently:

Skin A Cat

Find as many different ways as possible of performing a simple action:

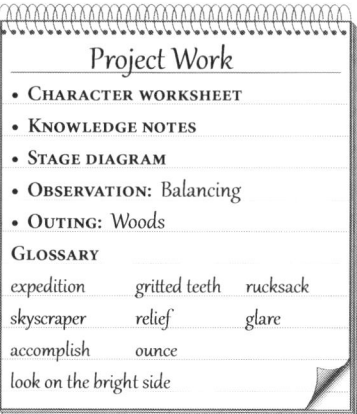

Project Work
- **Character worksheet**
- **Knowledge notes**
- **Stage diagram**
- **Observation:** Balancing
- **Outing:** Woods
- **Glossary**

expedition	gritted teeth	rucksack
skyscraper	relief	glare
accomplish	ounce	
look on the bright side		

- An actor takes the stage and mimes or acts feeding ducks at the park.
- Another actor takes the stage and feeds the ducks but does something different. If the ideas flow, continue. Otherwise, feed in suggestions.
- Differences could be physical. What do you feed the ducks? Where do you keep your duck food? How do you get the food to the ducks' beaks? How big are the ducks? How big are you? How many ducks are there?
- There might be differences of attitude. Is this a new experience or a daily habit? Is the food old and unwanted or special? Do you love the ducks? Admire them? Fear them? Are you disgusted by them? Jealous of them? Do you feed them joyfully or reluctantly? Cautiously or chaotically?
- Your actors will soon find that there are thousands of ways of feeding ducks, and that it is great fun finding new ones.
- Run through some other actions if you have time: choosing apples at the supermarket; milking a cow; changing a baby's nappy.
- Return to the key difference between **George** and **Wil** (as specified in the preamble). Ask Wil to perform one of the actions confidently and George with a lack of confidence.

Variation: Adverb Game

Write as many interesting adverbs as you can think of on pieces of paper (or download the adverb cards from the web page which accompanies this book) and put them in a hat. Choose an action; actors in turn pick an adverb from the hat and perform the action appropriately. Award points for every correct guess (to both guesser and performer) or play in teams, challenging each team to see how many adverbs they can guess in a minute.

Alternatively, one player picks an adverb, and teammates have to guess what it is by calling out actions to be performed in that manner.

Into the Scene

Finally, identify key moments where George and Wil might do the same thing differently:

- first seeing the river
- first seeing the log
- stepping onto the log
- seeing the bag left behind

Teamwork

Despite their differences, George and Wil must work together. Ultimately, they succeed; though hampered by his nervousness, George does not fall in, and though exasperated, Wil does manage to coax George across.

Practise the dynamic between the characters with a collaboration game in which one (who is blindfolded) must follow the other's instructions to complete a task.

❋ HOLD THE ENDING ❋

*S*hort scenes written specially for exam or festival performance often end with a dramatic line. The words hang enticingly in the air for a few seconds before dissolving. Point this out to your actors and show them how to let the words hang by 'holding the ending'. Whatever their final reaction or expression (here, Wil's might be anger or despair, George's might be regret or horror), they should not exactly freeze but hold onto the feeling so that the drama stays alive. Maintain eye contact, stay still, breathe and think about the words that have just been spoken. After a couple of seconds, break eye contact and come out of character. Holding the ending adds a final flourish to a scene and strengthens its impact.

- **Blindfold Robot Wars**
  Pair up into Georges and Wils. George is the robot, and Wil is the controller. Robots, blindfolded, stand in the centre of a large open space. Scattered around are light plastic balls or scrunched up paper. Following instructions from their controllers, robots move around until they locate a ball and pick it up. They must throw the ball at another robot. Three hits and a robot dies. If you only have two actors, George has to hit you.
- **Blindfold Minefield**
  The blindfolded actor stands in the middle of the room, instructor on the edge. Scattered around are objects to be collected and objects to be avoided (mines). Blindfolded actor, following instructions, has to collect a given number of objects in a certain time without stepping on a mine.
- **Blindfold Drawing**
  The blindfolded actor is given a pen and paper and must draw the shape described to him by his partner.

Further Ideas

- Each actor can practise 'crossing the river' (walking along a line on the floor) with a book on his head or carrying an egg and spoon. If the book or the egg slide off, he has fallen into the river. Focus attention on what happens in the body when you are trying hard to keep your balance and include that physicality in the performance.
- Find a wall or beam that your actors can walk along and use it in a rehearsal. Use the real 'log' to work out all the business with George's feet.
- Ask your actors to invent circumstances surrounding the scene. What is this expedition they are on? Are they alone, or is someone waiting for them somewhere? What is the weather like? What time is it?

Source

This scene has been adapted from a fantasy novel published in 2003. Although the adaptation is quite close, it might be useful to read the original. Your students might enjoy the whole book, especially if they have a taste for magic and enjoy a crazy narrative.

Nick's Wants and Obstacles

Ask **Nick** to take the stage. He is in a dark and narrow rocky gully. His life has been threatened, and he wants to find the wizard Romanov. What's stopping him? He might answer, 'I don't know where Romanov is'; 'I don't know where I am'; 'I can't see where I'm going.'

These are Nick's obstacles. What will he do to overcome them? 'I'll use my instinct to guess where Romanov is'; 'I won't worry about where I am'; 'I'll feel my way along.' These are Nick's actions. Ask him to take the stage and play the three actions, without words at first. The obstacles are daunting, but his want is powerful, and he battles on.

Nick grasps what he thinks is a snake. His actions are swamped by the new circumstances. Initially, he is terrified. What does he now want? To escape (but it is dark)? To protect himself from attack (but he is unarmed)?

Then he hears a voice, more terrified than his. What does he now want? What new obstacles have arisen?

Project Work

- CHARACTER WORKSHEET
- KNOWLEDGE NOTES
- STAGE DIAGRAM
- OBSERVATION: *Elephants' trunks*
- OUTING: *Zoo*
- ART: *Elephant collage; setting*

GLOSSARY

parallel world	dab	harness
governor	shriek	reared up
enlist	panther	hind
encounter	squeal	
grope	trample	

✳ WHAT DO YOU WANT? ✳

A character in a play does or says something: why? In *An Actor Prepares* (1936), Stanislavsky writes that the circumstances at any given moment provide a character with a *zadacha*. The question of how to translate this Russian word into English has greatly vexed theatre practitioners. Objective? Intention? Motivation? Task? *Zadacha* is in fact an everyday Russian word that means 'mathematical problem' – Stanislavsky said he had this sense of the word in mind when he chose it. Being wedged in a crevasse certainly gives an elephant a problem!

Your young actors must make a connection between the outer world of their actions and the inner world of their feelings. What do their characters want? What do they do to get it?

Want is an excellent word to use with young actors as it needs no explanation or jargon. I want to be a happy person; I want to finish my maths homework; I want a Twix.

Your young actors will know how a child can want something with his or her entire being. Wanting can be visceral, primeval, all-consuming. The tantrumming three-year-old is in complete meltdown because he is not getting what he WANTS! Challenge your actors to find similar intensity and power in their character's efforts to get what they want.

Mini's Wants and Obstacles

Ask **Mini** to take the stage and absorb herself in her situation. What does she want? To escape the dark paths by going back the way she came. What's stopping her? Also that she can't see and doesn't know where she is, but mainly that she can't turn around and is 'not good at going backwards.'

Though Mini's want is powerful, she is going neither forwards nor backwards. Has she given up, or is she still battling her obstacles? What are her actions? Waiting? Thinking? Panicking?

How do Mini's wants change when Nick crashes into her? She puts herself at his mercy and now wants his help. What new obstacles are there? That he might be hostile? That he might not want to help her? What can she do to overcome hostility or unwillingness? These are her new actions.

GAME: WHAT'S STOPPING YOU?

This simple exercise demonstrates how wants and obstacles produce action, the essential component of drama.

- Place an object (a trophy, say) in the playing space. Tell an actor to play the following silent scene: you want the trophy.
- You might get a grand display of desire towards the trophy. But what simple action can he perform? (He can go and get the trophy.)
- A getting-the-trophy scene is unlikely to be dramatic. Introduce a series of obstacles, and repeat the scene. The trophy might be red hot or superglued to the table; it might be fragile or it might turn anybody who touches it into a jellyfish. The setting might be a lurching ship or a field in the middle of a hurricane. The actor might be extremely drunk, a recovering trophy thief or suffering from twitching disease. Whatever obstacle you introduce, you'll have a struggle – and therefore drama.
- Introduce a second character who wants the trophy to stay where it is: he's a guard in a museum; he's trying to break the world record for trophy watching; he's waiting for lightning to strike it so he can travel to the future. That character is now the obstacle. The actors can add dialogue.
- Ask classmates for the outcome they would like to see: which character succeeds in getting what he wants? What will be more interesting – if he succeeds easily or narrowly succeeds? Deciding this beforehand removes the competitiveness that can hamper improvisations and gives the 'loser' the freedom to invest energy in playing his character's defeat.

Character: Mini

Have a look at page 27 for some ideas on creating animal characters. If you decide to give Mini a trunk, focus on its quality of movement. Challenge your actor to make her arm as trunk-like as possible in the way it curls, hangs, twitches, swings and grasps.

Mini's noises (shrieks, squeals and trumpets) are specified in the stage directions. Practise elephant noises on their own at first, then look for places where you can elephantilise Mini's words.

As she develops her character, encourage your actor to do independent research by watching nature videos or, best of all, by taking a trip to the zoo.

THE FINAL SNORE

by Clare Price ✳ Acting Anthology page 144

Settings

The action starts in a boys' dormitory, where **Oliver** and **Chris** share a bunk bed. Next they leave the dormitory and walk along a corridor past a teacher's room. The final part of the scene takes place in the great hall.

How – without any set or lighting – might your actors convey the shift from one location to the next?

- **FREEDOM OF MOVEMENT**
  The dormitory must be quite crowded, so even when Oliver and Chris get out of bed, they have little space to move around. In the corridor they walk more freely, although the space is still narrow. In the great hall they can move freely. Practise walking with small steps, medium steps and large steps. Take gestures such as looking at a watch, pulling up a sock or pointing at something and see if your actors can find three different levels, from small/contained to expansive/free.

- **VOLUME**
  In the dormitory, other boys might wake up if Oliver and Chris are noisy. In the corridor, they can be a little louder, although there is a danger that their teacher will hear them. In the great hall they can be noisier still (but must be careful not to attract attention). Practise speaking a phrase or sentence at three different levels, from voiced whisper to normal volume.

- **SPEED**
  The dormitory is dark, and the boys need to use a torch. There may be a little light in the corridor, although they still use the torch. In the great hall they switch the main lights on. When they struggle to see, the boys will move slowly and cautiously. In the dim corridor, they will move with a little more confidence, and in the great hall visibility is not a problem. Practise different movements (putting a shoe on, walking, opening a trapdoor) at three different speeds.

- **TENSION**
  Overall, the boys are extremely restricted in the dormitory, so there will be a lot of tension in their bodies as they restrain their movements and voice. By the time they reach the hall, they are more relaxed (although there is still plenty to cause them tension).

DORMITORY, CORRIDOR OR HALL?

Consolidate by playing a quick guessing game: give each boy a simple action and ask them to choose (secretly) one of the three locations. They perform the action: can you (or classmates) guess which location they are in?

Project Work

- **CHARACTER WORKSHEET**
- **KNOWLEDGE NOTES**
- **STAGE DIAGRAM**
- **OBSERVATION:** Moving in the dark
- **ART:** The final moment
- **WRITING:** Diary of last night

GLOSSARY

dormitory	gestures	prise
unconvinced	night rounds	hatch
shower block	intently	resolve
stealthily	wild goose chase	

118

Battle of Wills

Play this scene as a literal tussle between the two boys. This exercise will work best if you have a large room:

- The boys stand face to face at one end of the room. Oliver has his back to the wall. He wants to get past Chris and across the room to reach something enticing (you could fix a bag of sweets to the opposite wall).
- Chris wants to keep Oliver where he is (or to push him back to where he started). They should not be crossing the room and will be in trouble if they are caught. The outcome is that Chris fails; Oliver crosses the room.
- First, play the exercise without words. Include moments when Chris's pushing does stop Oliver's progress.
- Now they improvise some simple dialogue. Oliver explains why it is important to get the sweets. Chris tries to persuade him it is a bad idea (by frightening Oliver, begging him, threatening him, and so on). At times, Chris's words do halt Oliver's progress – but he gets there eventually.
- Finally, play the exercise using the actual dialogue. Can the boys work out when to push hard and when to relent? When they play the scene conventionally, their memory of pushing against each other should add impetus and antagonism to the performance.
- The exercise should have opened up all sorts of differences between Chris and Oliver – the one more cautious, circumspect and practical, and the other more foolhardy, intense and imaginative.

Situation

This is the third night in a row that the strange tapping noise has prompted Oliver to wake Chris up. Last night both boys got out of bed and checked the shower block. Hot-seat your boys to get the story of what happened. They'll be talking off the top of their heads, so allow for different accounts and work towards an agreement. When you have it, re-enact last night's events.

WHY DOES CHRIS GET UP?

There are all sorts of reasons for Chris to stay in bed, but he reluctantly decides to get up and find out what is making the tapping noise. Why does he make this decision? Out of sympathy for Oliver? Out of curiosity or excitement? Or so that the mystery is solved and he can get to sleep?

Further Ideas

- Mr Wieland is an important figure. Both boys worry about being caught by him, and his entrance at the end marks the scene's climax. In a quiet moment, your actors could draw that final moment.
- Use a stand-in so that the boys share a clear point of focus.
- Real torches would be a good hand prop – they are not cumbersome and would add to the atmosphere. The boys could wear dressing gowns. Real trainers are worth considering if Chris can easily slip them on and off.
- Spend some time working out how to do the trainer in the well. Whether or not you use a real trainer, your actors should practise watching it disappear down into the deep hole.

The Forks

Lily spends the entire scene and **Alice** spends a portion of it cleaning forks. It is an important piece of business – just about the only physical action in the scene – and it would be a good idea to devote some time to working out exactly how to do it so that your students are making a conscious acting choice (rather than performing an automatic action).

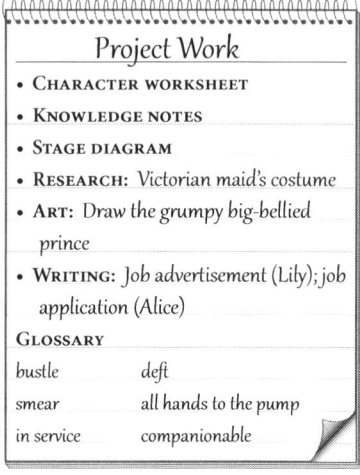

Project Work
- CHARACTER WORKSHEET
- KNOWLEDGE NOTES
- STAGE DIAGRAM
- RESEARCH: Victorian maid's costume
- ART: Draw the grumpy big-bellied prince
- WRITING: Job advertisement (Lily); job application (Alice)

GLOSSARY

bustle	deft
smear	all hands to the pump
in service	companionable

- First, establish with your actors that there are lots of different ways to clean a fork. Give them each a cloth and challenge them to come up with different fork cleaning actions. They can vary the speed, weight and rhythm of the action and their attitude towards it as well as the position of arms, head and body. Have a look at the game 'Skin a Cat' on page 114 for more ideas on finding variations of a single action.
- Next make a list of adverbs (or download the adverb cards from the web page which accompanies this book) and pick one at random. Challenge your actors to polish a fork luxuriously, cruelly or sloppily.
- Now examine the circumstances that lie behind Lily's fork polishing. Help your actors to make a list all of the facts you know about Lily's situation:
  - Lily has been polishing forks very slowly for an hour. She has only finished a few.
  - She is very new to this job and is trying hard to do it well.
  - She is very tired.
  - She is naive and tearful and lacks confidence.
  - Alice, her superior, is monitoring her work.
  - Alice has worked there for a year and is confident and knowledgeable.
  - Mr. Keeling, Alice's boss's boss (perhaps the butler?), does not like smears on the cutlery.
  - The prince is coming to dine with the master of the house tomorrow night.
- This last circumstance is the key plot point of the scene and the reason the forks must be polished now and finished soon. This looming event puts a great deal of pressure on both Lily and Alice. The job must be done quickly and well: the stakes are high.
- Every circumstance in the list adds to the pressure on the polishing and the tension in the scene. Play the opening few lines and encourage Lily to feel a physical release of tension when Alice praises her work.

> ## ❋ COSTUME ❋
>
> Only use an item of costume if it is vital to the story, will significantly enhance the performance and will not cause your actor stress or affect the timing of the exam. If necessary, rehearse with costumes (and props) but take them out for the exam performance.
>
> Facial expressions are crucial, so avoid headwear that obscures any part of the face. Long hair must be tied back. Have hair bands, slides and grips available in every class and on exam day.
>
> It is a very good idea for girls playing a period scene (one set before 1950) to wear a practice skirt when rehearsing and performing. This is a long (ankle-length), loose, unpleated skirt, usually black, that gives the impression of period costume and encourages a less modern way of moving. Practice skirts can be bought new, hunted down in charity shops or home-made. An elasticated waistband means skirts can be worn over trousers and slipped on and off in seconds.
>
> If exam performances include a quick costume change, ensure your students remain decent. See also the notes on props in LAMDA Exams on page 41.

- What happens in Lily's face and body a little further on when Alice is dismayed at how few forks Lily has polished?

THE FLOODGATES OPEN

That the tension inside Lily has been building up is evident when she bursts into tears. You will help Lily play this moment convincingly if she has been on the verge of tears in the preceding lines, from the point where Alice criticises her work. Trying not to cry creates physical tension, especially if Lily can feel her tear ducts prickling, her throat constricting and the blood rushing to her face.

Have some fun practising this moment off the text. Doing so will take any embarrassment factor out of the tears. It's only pretending, after all, and your actors will benefit from some crying practice.

Provide a simple scenario in which A is teaching B to do something. B is trying her best but getting it hopelessly wrong and eventually breaking down. If the activity is a foolishly simple one, you'll increase the enjoyment:

- Tie your shoelaces
- Put your gloves on
- Perform 'Heads, Shoulders, Knees and Toes'

Vary A's attitude from indulgent to exasperated, from kind to angry to explore how the different dynamics change the drama. Which one makes for the more entertaining scene? Which one more closely matches the dynamic of the full scene?

To help B get upset, give A a balloon. Every time B says or does something stupid, A can hit her on the head. You could also rehearse the scene with Alice wielding a balloon. Afterwards, give it to Lily so that she can have her revenge!

Accents

Parlour maids in a Victorian house would not be well spoken, so encourage your actors to use accents that suggest they come from lower-class families. If they are dropping *t*'s and turning *-ing* into *-in'* and *th* into *f*, make sure that they do so clearly, strongly and consistently so that clarity is not sacrificed.

Source

This scene is adapted from a short story in E Nesbit's *The Book of Dragons* (1901). The conversation between **George** and **Jane** comes close to the beginning. Your actors might enjoy this charming tale by a much-loved children's author. There are two other Nesbit adaptations in the Acting Anthology.

Costume

It is an icy December night, and both children are heavily wrapped up. The opening lines specify various outlandish pieces of costume, but too many layers will hamper your actors' performance and put them in danger of overheating.

You could mime the costume altogether. It is clear what the children are wearing, since each describes the other's clothes. Alternatively, you could find a piece or two that gives the actors the sensation of being muffled up – and is suggestive of heavy clothing – without making them too warm.

> ### Project Work
> - **CHARACTER WORKSHEET**
> - **KNOWLEDGE NOTES**
> - **STAGE DIAGRAM**
> - **RESEARCH:** Body's response to cold; life in cold climates
> - **OBSERVATION:** Being cold
> - **OUTING:** Temperature drop
> - **ART:** Book cover
> **GLOSSARY**
>
> | | | |
> |---|---|---|
> | cut a tooth | sealskin | mischief |
> | cape | constellation | |
> | muff | gloomy | |

Never Been So Cold

Your actors must convey the cold through body language and appropriate movement. Generate ideas by setting some research and observation tasks:

- Your actors should try to observe themselves when they are cold.
- If it is cool, stand outside in T-shirts. If the ground is clean and dry, take shoes and socks off. Stand for a minute or two, allowing yourselves to get cold and watching how the body responds. Imagine it colder – a heavy sky, an icy wind chilling your skin, snow falling on your face.
- If self-observation is not feasible, watch footage of people living in wintry conditions. Look for documentaries set in very cold places.
- Share ideas about what happens physically when you are cold. Your body switches into warm-itself-up mode:
  - You try to keep the warmth in by hunching your shoulders.
  - You generate heat by jiggling yourself around.
  - Your muscles jiggle automatically (you shiver and your jaw chatters).
  - Hairs on your skin prick up to trap warm air (you get goose pimples).
  - Your body takes warm blood away from its extremities and into its centre (your fingers and toes go numb).
  - Your face demands extra warm blood (your cheeks are flushed and your nose goes red).
  - Your heart pumps more blood into your nostrils so that they can warm up the air you're breathing in. As a result, the mucus machine goes into overdrive and you get a runny nose.

- Whenever you are rehearsing this scene, refer back to the list above. Find moments for your actors to imagine or express these bodily responses to their icy surroundings.

The Setting

At first George and Jane focus only on their immediate surroundings – the garden of their house and the failed firework.

When they climb the fence, they gaze at what lies beyond their little world. Their attention alights briefly on their neighbour's garden and the Crystal Palace before they gaze at the horizon and then at the distant stars. Finally, George's focus switches to the North Pole, and they set off on their adventure.

Your actors should know exactly where they are looking and when. If the exam will take place in the room you rehearse in, nominate spots around the room – plug sockets, clocks, chips in the paint – to be the Crystal Palace, the Aurora Borealis and so on. If the exam will be in an unfamiliar room, make decisions about the directions the actors will look in.

Characters

The children's differing attitudes to what they are looking at reveal much about their different characters and the relationship between them. When Jane stares at the lights in the sky, she imagines a glowing fairy world. George quickly dismisses her ideas and provides a rational explanation from his schoolbook. He trumps his sister's imaginative speculations with his facts. Even when his grasp of those facts is shaky, he knows that he knows more than Jane.

Jane does not fight back or get upset when her brother rubbishes her ideas. When she looks again at the Aurora Borealis, does she still see fairy-trees? Is her wonder undimmed? Or has George explained the fairies away?

George establishes several times that he is more grown-up than his 'kid' sister. He considers himself grown up enough to emulate his adventure-book heroes by going on a voyage to the North Pole. Jane, captivated by all the mystery and wonder around her, excitedly agrees. Both want to discover the world – he to demonstrate his courage, she other to experience its magic.

Ask your actors to create a still image of their characters gazing out towards the North Pole. Can they find a facial expression that conveys their attitude towards the voyage they are about to go on? Can they come up with a tableau that tells the whole story of these characters and the scene?

- Make a frozen picture that could be a book cover for this story. Take a photo of it, show your actors and discuss how it could be refined.
- If you have classmates, invite them to come and refine the still image by moulding George and Jane.
- Print out copies of the photo and ask your actors to incorporate it into a cover design for a new edition of The Ice Dragon.
- Continue your work on the children's attitudes (and also on expressing coldness through body language) by telling the whole story of this scene in a series of tableaux.

The Background

The source for this scene is the end of the second chapter of Marryat's historical novel for children, written in 1847 but set two hundred years earlier. The adaptation is close (although **Jacob** is over sixty years old in the book).

Edward (thirteen) and his siblings are recently orphaned; their father was killed fighting for the king, and their mother died of grief. As Colonel Beverley left for war, Jacob promised that he would watch over the family.

Earlier this afternoon, Jacob overheard Roundhead soldiers plotting to burn down Arnwood, where they think the king might be hiding. He raced there and smuggled the children out to his cottage. He then returned to Arnwood and has just watched the soldiers torch it. (Aunt Judith, who initially refused to budge, gets out but dies in a fall from a horse shortly afterwards.) Jacob is decent, loyal and fond of the Beverley children.

Project Work

- CHARACTER WORKSHEET
- KNOWLEDGE NOTES
- STAGE DIAGRAM
- RESEARCH: Roundheads and Cavaliers
- ART: Arnwood in happier times
- GLOSSARY

Civil War	undergrowth	forfeited
Cavalier	dense	Woe to
Royalist	nodding	Covenanter
Roundhead	Leveler	vengeance
gamekeeper	contrary	rash
a force to be reckoned with		

Find active ways to help your actors internalise their characters' history:
- Ask Jacob to describe the events of this afternoon. As Jacob narrates, Edward and classmates can help him act the events out.
- Improvise a scene in which Colonel Beverley, about to go off to war, entrusts Jacob with the job of looking after the children.
- Edward draws his family at home at Arnwood in happy times.
- Edward picks a prop and weaves a childhood memory around it. He brings the memory to life by acting it out, with Jacob's help.
- Hot-seat Edward and Jacob together. Can they remember a time when they played together in the woods?
- Ask Edward to find (in a magazine or online) a picture of a house that could be Arnwood. What are his favourite and least favourite rooms?

Up In Flames

The burning house is a key point of focus for both characters during the scene. What goes through each boy's mind as he watches the glow between the trees?

Each actor comes up with a happy memory of the house. Make the visual details as vivid as possible, so that the memory can be quickly recalled.

When you rehearse, ask each actor to recall his happy memory as he looks into the distance. Can they surround the mental image with flames, as though the whole imagined scene were a burning photograph? The vision fills Jacob with fear and Edward with anger.

Atmosphere and Tension

The forest is dark and frosty. To be discovered would be terrible, so Jacob must be quiet. He must get back to the cottage as quickly as he can. The wood is full of fire and death. Arnwood is only a mile and a half away. Does Jacob smell smoke? Hear the crackle of burning timbers and the whoops of soldiers?

Inside the cottage, Edward has been waiting for Jacob with no idea of when he will return. He has been been left in charge of his three siblings. He would rather have stayed and defended Arnwood, but Jacob persuaded him not to abandon his little sisters. His childhood home and future inheritance are going up in flames. The woods are overrun by people who want him dead.

All of these circumstances add tension to Jacob and Edward, which both actors should carry into the scene.

See-sawing Status

Edward, the social superior, naturally has higher status than Jacob. Jacob, no social rebel, accepts this. Yet this is Jacob's plan and his territory. His comment on Edward's youthful rashness suggests that he is the older of the two.

Ask your actors when they think their character is the one in charge. How would the person in charge use his voice and body to show authority?

- Freeze the scene at an appropriate moment. Who is in charge? Is it obvious from the frozen image? Invite classmates to come and improve the image by remoulding Edward and Jacob.
- Play a quick game: you shout out a setting and two characters. Two actors must take the stage and create a tableau in which the characters clearly have different status. The audience have to figure out which character is which and who has the higher and the lower status.

See pages 80–81 for further ideas on status.

❋ SEVEN LEVELS OF TENSION ❋

*H*ow do actors create tension? Partly through the imagination. If they believe that things could go either way, and that which way they go is a matter of life and death, then their words and actions gain force. They listen intently, speak urgently and put soul into their actions.

Tension in a scene will hook in an audience. If the stakes are high, the audience shares the characters' anxieties about the outcome and follows closely to see which way things will go.

Creating tension is also physical. Identify what circumstances create tension and allow them to affect the body, breathing, face and voice. Is it cold? Must we be quiet? Am I in pain? Am I confused? Are we hiding? Is there danger nearby? Any of these factors would cause the body to tense up.

The French acting teacher Jacques LeCoq (1921–99) first proposed seven levels of tension, ranging from close to death to close to asphyxia. The idea has been widely taken up.

1. Drained (no tension; unable to move)
2. Relaxed (able to move, but aimlessly)
3. Neutral (perfect movement, no wasted energy)
4. Alert ('What's in the room?')
5. Suspense ('Is there a bomb in the room?')
6. Passion ('There IS a bomb in the room!')
7. Panic ('The bomb is about to go off!')

Different teachers give different names to the seven levels. Use ones that help your youngsters to transform themselves. Take short scenes or études and play them at different levels of tension.

Source

This scene is taken from a children's play written in 2009 for the Darwin200 project. The play is a two-hander, though **Charlie** and **Fitz** play other characters (including Charles Darwin and the *Beagle*'s Captain Fitzroy). The zany scene is typical of Mick Gordon's wildly energetic play.

Project Work
- CHARACTER WORKSHEET
- KNOWLEDGE NOTES
- STAGE DIAGRAM
- RESEARCH: *Darwinism*
- OBSERVATION: *Dogs and fish*
- ART: *The Ride of Your Life*

GLOSSARY

evolution	mutant
at your service	Belisha beacon

The Comedy

Comedy works best when the stakes are high. Although it might seem a lightweight scene, your students should throw a lot of energy into the playing. It will be easier for Charlie, whose state of crisis is obvious. Fitz will need to find ways of matching Charlie's energy as he moves from gloating delight to horror, guilt and regret.

- **MERMAN**

  Charlie has a fish's lower parts. Work out how his movement is changed by this transformation. Are there times when he forgets he doesn't have legs and falls over? He is angry at Fitz – how is his anger affected by the fact that he is physically powerless? It is clear from the last line of the scene that Charlie cannot walk. What is his reaction when he looks down at himself? What is Fitz's opinion of Charlie's transformation?

- **STATUS**

  Before this scene, Charlie has had the authority in the relationship. Fitz accepts that Charlie is his master and soaks up the continual verbal (and sometimes physical) abuse. Although Fitz idolises his mother (an Irish Wolfhound), he despises the part of himself that is descended from his father (a Beagle). His self-image is greatly impaired by his purple flashing bum. He has to agree with Charlie's view that he is an ugly mutant.

  Now, though, Fitz's status has jumped a notch or two. He is intelligent and handsome with a normal bum. How will he express his new self-confidence? How will Charlie respond to Fitz's attempts to occupy a higher step on the status ladder? What response had Fitz anticipated?

- **SURPRISE!**

  Charlie is incandescent with rage. He means to find out what Fitz has done and make him undo it. However, he keeps getting distracted by the amazing transformation in Fitz. Although his anger is real, he has to keep remembering to be angry. Fitz is basking in pleasure with his evolved self but is also distracted by Charlie's transformation. There is also a dawning realisation that he has done something 'really, really bad'.

- **DON'T BE ANGRY**

  Spend some time looking at the strategies Fitz employs to defuse Charlie's anger:

- Show the bright side
- Make a full confession
- Downgrade the wrongdoing
- Plead ignorance
- Appeal to the emotions

It should be highly amusing to watch Fitz trying all these different tactics, each as ineffective as the last.

You could do a quick improvisation game in which A is furious with B, who has done something terribly wrong. B tries the strategies listed above (fed in or prompted by you in any order) to defuse A's anger, but to no avail.

Animal Transformations: Fitz

Fitz is a dog, but a very human sort of a dog. He sings Irish ditties and talks nineteen to the dozen. All Charlie heard up to now were barks and yaps, but now Fitz can speak human. He is handsome and wears a hat (the source specifies that he's dressed like Fred Astaire).

Ask your actors to come up with a list of things that dogs do (keep it active by asking them to show you as well as or instead of telling you). Give the exercise focus by asking them to attach everything to an emotion or circumstance:

- When they are curious they sniff things.
- When they are angry or frightened they growl.
- When they are happy they wag their tail.
- When they are listening they put their head to one side.

Expand the list. Can your Fitz actor find any moments in the scene where these emotions or circumstances come into play? Could these be canine moments for him?

Animal Transformations: Charlie

Charlie is fully human… except for the fish's lower half that Fitz has accidentally caused him to evolve. How can your actor make his legs look and behave as though they belong to a fish? Can he create an element of surprise when he first removes the duvet and reveals his lower half? What position will he take on the stage? Can he hop around upright at all?

Challenge your actor to find ways in which his lower half might express emotion, especially anger. Might his tail thrash or curl?

Work, too, on the 'strange fishy movements' Charlie's mouth makes as he hears what exactly Fitz has done. Is this a coincidence, or is the fishiness spreading upwards?

I Wanted to Explain…

Whenever a thought is incomplete or cut off, as it is in Fitz's fourth-to-last speech, the actor should know what he was going to say. Fitz's main purpose in going back in time was to evolve himself to speak human so that he could explain evolution to Charlie.Not only would this prevent Charlie from getting expelled from school (he must get a Gold Star for his science homework) but it would also help Charlie (an orphan) to understand that he has a family after all: since all living things are related, Fitz is his family.

Tell Me More!

More than half of the sentences spoken by **A** during this scene are questions. A's avid curiosity and continual interrogation of **B** drive this scene forward as the mystery of the ghost in the loft deepens.

Why is A so fascinated? He might be a generally curious person. Or if it has been quiet in the shop, B might be the first company he has had all day. He might have a particular interest in the occult. He might be pursuing a second career as an investigative journalist. There are many possibilities; encourage your student to make an actor's choice so that what A wants – to know all the details of the story – is rooted in character and/or situation.

For much of the scene, A is hanging on B's every word. In rehearsal, ask A to repeat the last word or couple of words of B's line before starting his own.

B: I'll take them all.
A: All! Are you researching a book?
B: No. I think my house is haunted.
A: Haunted! Really!

Picking up on B's words in this way will encourage A to listen hard. What emotions come with those echoes? The exercise works well if books are down but only just, so that A is not yet fully familiar with B's lines.

For variety, use numbered cards to explore levels of fascination. At which moments is his fascination level at 10? Where does it dip?

If your actor likes words, ask him to look up *fascinated* in a thesaurus. When is A intrigued, absorbed, spellbound, agog and so on?

You could also try colouring A's fascination, metaphorically and literally. He might be fascinated in a positive sense – fascinated and delighted – or in a negative sense – fascinated and appalled. Write the word 'fascinated' in the centre of a piece of paper and add synonyms around it. What colour does he instinctively feel belongs to belongs to each synonym? Ask him to colour the words, then to add coloured splodges or highlights to his script.

QUESTION GAMES

Play a questioning game with A and B to give off-the-text practice at the dynamic between them in the scene: The first two here can be played in a pair, the third (and its variations) needs a group. A time limit will add impetus.

- **GUESS WHO!**
  A classic board game in which A asks yes/no questions in order to discover by a process of elimination which face is on B's chosen card. Buy the original or make your own version.

- TWENTY QUESTIONS
  A asks yes/no questions in an attempt to discover, by a process of elimination, which famous person B is thinking of.
- FOREHEAD DETECTIVE
  Write down names of famous people on pieces of paper and fix them to students' foreheads (so everyone can see who everyone else is). They circulate; each must find out who he is by asking yes/no questions.
  - VARIATION ONE
    If you have enough students, choose people who are part of a famous couple or a double-act; the goal is to find your partner.
  - VARIATION TWO
    Instead of written names, use pictures of people cut in half. The goal is to find your other half.

Under the Spell

Is it really A's questioning that drives the scene? If A is spellbound, B is casting the spell – or rather the net, for at the end A falls right into B's trap.

There is something of the hypnotist about B as he draws A into his spooky story. Each of his lines provides just one piece of the jigsaw and ends with a new mystery, a hint that there is something he hasn't told A yet: 'some very strange things'; 'and then there's the light'; 'Then it spoke to me'. Lured by these little hints, A is desperate to know more. B's final trick is to provide A with a code to crack. A takes the bait.

Tweak the dynamic between the characters to make B's enticements the driving force of the scene:

- GAMES
  Any of the games above can be modified to emphasise B's drip-drip supply of information in answer to A's questions. Encourage B to be as mysterious and all-knowing as possible.
- MAGIC
  Ask B (as a homework task) to learn a magic trick – one that he thinks A won't be able to figure out – and to show the class at the next lesson.
- HYPNOSIS
  A and B can improvise a hypnotism scene with B as the hypnotist. A has a habit he wants to be cured of or a past life he wants to discover.
- FORTUNE TELLER
  Alternatively, B could tell A's fortune. They can improvise a scene in which A asks lots of questions and B gives mysterious half-answers.
- FALL INTO MY TRAP
  Give B a bag of sweets and play the scene. Every time B supplies new information, he puts a sweet in A's hand. A gobbles it up. Every time B ends a line, he waves a sweet enticingly in front of A. A plays as though he is starving hungry. (Ensure hands are clean and there are no allergies).

Further Idea

The scene in the loft is vividly described by B. Stage it. During quiet time in class (or at home), draw the loft encounter.

INDEX

23203680R00078

Printed in Great Britain
by Amazon